PRAISE FOR
STRUT YOUR STUFF

"The Emergency Department is often a window to the world in which we live and a gateway for those in pain and suffering. As a physician, I have the privilege of comforting complete strangers for a brief moment at a very critical time in their lives. I have learned that emotional pain is often a catalyst for growth and maturity.

Raquel's skill to heal with words parallels my devotion to my male and female patients. STRUT YOUR STUFF is a compelling, introspective journey of one's life from the seeds of the roots of conflict to the blossom of one's true purpose. It is reminiscent of one's passage through mortality, as we reflect on our past, unveiling the very conflicts suppressed in our subconscious that mold the very spiritual persons we choose to become. Raquel's Strut Chart exercises ingeniously align and bring into consciousness our fragmented pasts, giving us the courage to be, to truly live and to experience our best selves.

Her ability to share these vital steps and some of her pain continues to touch many women and the men in their lives. Raquel's dedication to assisting others to empower themselves is evidenced by her weekly inspirational columns, leadership conferences for women and her dedication to raising funds and awareness for the "Lost Boys of Sudan " .

Strut Your Stuff is really a guide to power, purpose and position for any woman or man with the courage to change."

-Maxime Alix Gilles, MD Board Certified Emergency
Physician and Author

PRAISE FOR
STRUT YOUR STUFF

⸎

"The title of the book says it all! Raquel Eatmon vividly illustrates how to confidently 'Strut Your Stuff'. Each chapter contains words of experience and wisdom that will transform your outlook, your thought process and your life. The author uses unique sections such as "Conjured Courage", "Unwriting History" and many others to guide readers toward personal accountability and the freedom to know and love ones self. Raquel draws upon personal experiences with friends, relatives and her successful career as a journalist and motivational speaker to highlight the fact that transforming our lives is a personal choice and is available to each and every one of us. There is no doubt, readers will learn life changing tools that will make them more peaceful, more productive, and more poised to confidently strut their stuff."

~Stacey Bell
Television News Anchor
New York, NY

"Strut Your Stuff is a compelling book abundant with information that stimulates your inner voice. Raquel Eatmon, your spiritual tour guide, takes you on a personal journey of exploration and self examination. You will discover how to get passed the hurt, learn to love, forgive and move forward in life. Through the power of prayer we can prevail over any obstacles and become victors in life. By following Raquel's lessons of enlightenment, we learn to reach our powerful potential that God has graciously placed in all of us!"

~Minister Stephanie Wilson Halfacre,
Inspirational Speaker and Author of
DreamQuest A Journey of Significant Vision

Strut Your Stuff

PRINCIPLES IN PURPOSE, POWER, AND POSITION

RAQUEL EATMON

Madison:
Always follow your "gut" - your
truth is there.
Cheering for you.

Rising Media LLC ~ USA

For Kay and Murdies.

I am a better, stronger person because I have crossed paths with both of you. I am moved beyond words by God's mercy and how He has beautifully shown me much of who I am by way of the two of you. I have celebrated the best of times and endured the darkest of times with grace and love because you have somehow shown me the way. I adore you and I lift you in total love and reverence.

CONTENTS

PART One. Self-ReNew   21

1 WHERE'S MY STUFF?   23

2 RESONANT REFLECTION   43

3 PREFERENTIAL PARDON   63

ACKNOWLEDGMENTS

My decision to take on the heartfelt assignment of writing this book was a necessity, a call in my spirit, I needed to give birth to this book and yet, I had no idea how some of it would or could come together considering that it takes a team of esteemed people to push it into action. From the moment I put my pencil to paper (yes, I still write it out before typing it), a spiritual concourse of good people with good intentions showed up for this project and they have enormously supported my work and my dreams.

I am in a state of insurmountable gratitude to those who have made this book better through their insightful contributions (which I call blessings) and I'm also sincerely grateful for the people who make me better (which I call angels). I have had the extraordinary pleasure of traveling this cherished road with my editor, Liza Heinig. I'm appreciative for her patience, meticulous eye, and tremendous skill. She has challenged my mind and nourished my spirit with support and kindness. I knew how special she was after our first meeting when an earthquake rocked our lunch table and forced us to evacuate the building. She has been shaking things up in my life ever since! I am blessed to call this wonderful, strong, caring woman my friend.

My passion for sharing with people brings me great joy and with that comes unexpected friendships and thoughtful business associates. To Stu Halfacre and his lovely wife Stephanie, I'm graciously aware of their tenderheartedness for wanting to see other people live their own dreams. Thank you for the graphic support and publishing guidance.

Thank you to two women who contributed to the cover image of this book. Hairstylist, Angel Morris for the work and dedication that she brings to elevate self-esteem in teens and for her creative ability to assist women in feeling and looking good. To artist, Robbin Jackson, who's make-up credentials far exceeds the number of brushes in her travel glam bags (and that's a lot)- is another powerhouse who extends herself as a top-notch image consultant who is dedicated to empowerment.

I also wish to thank photographer Herb Bias for his patience as I changed my mind several times on the design of this book. I'm appreciative for our twenty-five year friendship and I admire his commitment to live a holistic life- which, in a spiritual sense, became apart of this book too.

There are many people who have wished me well along the way and I am so very thankful for their kindness and warm regards. From neighbors and colleagues to acquaintances and business associates, I thank you. I'm also deeply indebted to those who contributed to this project by way of their heartfelt endorsement or testimonial. I sincerely appreciate your thoughts and comments.

And to my dear, dear close friends who are extraordinarily special and supremely divine, I am elated to walk this path with each and every one of them.

I don't know where I would be without the love and prayers of my treasured friend and spiritual sister Diane Smith. Her display of genuine love has and continues to guide me to a stronger place in my own life. I thank her for whispering the truth to me and for always holding me accountable for my own "stuff". I love both her and Vanessa for not only the contributions they have deposited into my life but for what they have given to the world.

Roxanne Kaufman Elliott, my dear, red-shoe wearing friend, I wish every woman in the world had a Roxanne in her corner. My life was enhanced the day I met her. She has been a strong source of support, always asking how she can help and never asking for or expecting anything in return. I'm indebted to her and so inspired by her work and love for humanity.

I have a sisterhood of friends who really bring out the best in me, they are brilliant teachers, masterful listeners, and occasional comedians. I'm grateful for their support during my darker times and for their sincere celebrations during the good times. I must thank: Jana Katsuyama for the good and long, uplifting conversations with tea and chocolate. Marsha Bonhart for showing me glimpses of who I really am. Thank you for consistently reminding me to count my blessings and when things get too crazy, "breathe deeply into a paper bag". Stacey Lynn for being open to me during a very confusing time. Thank you for reminding me of courage and for demonstrating loyalty and commitment. Michelle Alexander for always accepting me just as I am and for continual love and support through the many years. Ladies, you all have layered my life with sheer delight, you have truly enriched my life and I'm deeply moved by your love for me. I love you all...greatly.

Judge Ron Spon and his wife Mary for their compassion and spiritual support. I'm truly grateful for our friendship and all of the prayers they have ordered into my life. They continue to remind me to move on God's call- not my own.

Tom Doerr, while we didn't work together on this project, he certainly has been a significant part of my professional and personal transformation. I am ever so thankful for his believing in me and encouraging me to follow my heart. He is a leader that rules with both Authority and Humility and I thank God for sending him my way.

I must extend my deepest gratitude to the many people who support my work by reading my newspaper column, attending my conferences and seminars. I'm in awe by all of the kindness they show me through handwritten letters, beautiful cards and thought-provoking emails. They remind me that I'm not traveling on this road alone.

Mostly, however, I want to acknowledge a small group of people who are very much a big part of my life: My family. Many thanks to my Uncle Vincent for his candid conversations and love. To my Aunt Sandy, thank you for our detailed conversations about family and history and many thanks to my cousin Sonia for the well wishes.

To my dear beautiful mother Kay, I appreciate and love her on so many different levels and I'm submerged in gratitude for the love that she has extended to me and for her strong commitment to see me rise above the many hardships I've encountered. She is a giving soul who has given me a great deal.

To my father and step-mother Bill and Shirley Pitts, all my love for making such a big splash in my life and all of the accountability calls of making sure I was still riding the wave. Their presence in my life humbles me and reminds me of how pure and magnificent God's grace is. Thank you for infusing such richness into my heart and my life. I love you.

And to my Grandmother, I am overjoyed to have been born into a family with her guidance and love. I'm grateful for her wit, straightforwardness, and power that she has demonstrated for me and through me. She will always be my "Superwoman". I love you.

Terry Farris, I am enormously thankful for his support during the earlier years in my life. While my childhood is long gone (ok, maybe not totally…), the support and effort he extended toward my education and overall development is still apart of me today. I love you Terry and much love to Jessica.

Pat McKinney, my beautifully spirited mother-in-law, has brought love, kindness, and prayer into my life when I needed it most. I'm forever grateful for our healthy lunches (minus the two baskets of bread) and easy conversations and I'm especially thankful to her for Dexter.

And last but certainly not least, there is a man who has witnessed my high times as well as the very low moments and he has never left my side. To my loving husband Dexter- who has wiped many tears from my face. I'm deeply inspired by his gracious heart and patient spirit to accept me as I am and love and respect me from that space. I'm reminded of all of the times I told him I wanted to write the book, he told me to do it. I'm reminded of the times when I told him I felt lost in my purpose and he told me to find it. And I can recall the times when I told him I felt like giving up and he held my hand and said, "Let's pray." Thank you, my dear sweet man, for seeing me through this project, thank you for loving me through this life and thank you for feeding me your awesome pancakes. I am so grateful that we have each other and I truly thank God for the amazing, bright spirit within you.

Je t'aime.

FOREWORD

One day as I sat in my office completely immersed in a stack of client work, my phone rang. I hesitated to answer it as I usually turn it off when I am in the "think tank", but for some reason I forgot to turn the ringer off that morning. So, I picked up the hand-set with my usual, "Good morning, this is Roxanne".

A lovely female voice started speaking, introducing herself and explaining that she was referred to me as a possible resource and connection for some power networking. We made arrangements to meet for coffee – or was it lunch? I don't remember. Actually, I don't remember the day, the month, the year or the time... all I remember is that when Raquel Eatmon and I met – I knew I was in the company of an old soul sister and friend that I just happen to be meeting for the first time... in this life.

We talked for hours.

I believe in the Universal Power of Alignment that brings old souls together. I believe in Red Shoes. I believe in the Magic of living a purposeful and intentional life. I believe in Raquel and the inner strength and power of Women. And I believe that we all need to give ourselves permission, and then the knowledge and power to… Strut Our Stuff.

Raquel has written an amazing book about that knowledge and power. Strut Your Stuff takes us on a journey of discovery, insight, deep personal reflection, tears, suspense, laughs, and prompts us into that ever so comforting nod of the head and wry smile when we read her words, learn of her stories, lessons and sorrows – and realize how much they sound like our own.

There is not a woman I have ever met that has not shared in at least some of the experiences that Raquel shares in this incredible journey, and the effects of these experiences and living our lives on everyone's else terms – and not our own.

From looking for and finding your "stuff"… learning how to stop apologizing… needing to please everyone… never saying "no"… being out of focus… being used… learning to forgive… learning to find your own genuine self… and creating the life that you were meant to live – with purpose and intention, grace, humility and humor – this is the journey Raquel takes us on.

And what a ride!

You will not be able to turn the pages fast enough as you begin reading, but take your time anyway. You don't want to miss any of the lessons or any of the wonderful stories Raquel shares – from her interview with Maya Angelou, to sponge busses, to "potty in a bucket" and all the other engaging and sometimes hilarious anecdotes of this incredible woman's story. Do the exercises, take the time to reflect on your life, your happiness and your true, genuine self. Are you everything you could and want to be? Raquel guides you through a process of reflection and self-discovery to truly understand – and perhaps for the first time - who you really are and who you are not.

So, ladies, here's to you and your Stuff. You will be charmed, enlightened, challenged and I dare say… changed, by this read. Then it's up to you to DO something with this gift. So start now, it's time to step up… put on your big girl shoes… and Strut Your Stuff!

Roxanne Kaufman Elliott
Founder and President, ProLaureate LTD
International Executive Leadership Coach
Executive Board Member, COSE
SOAR coach
Author of numerous business and leadership articles

PREFACE

This isn't a starting over book, it's a starting now book. What's done is done and you and I can choose whether to allow our past to paralyze and limit us or we can choose to use it as a powerful asset.

I don't believe in coincidence or luck, I believe in the powerful guide that is within us all, the same one that guided you to this very page. You are here because you're seeking something, you want something, you need something, you deserve something, whatever it is, whatever is gnawing at you or pleading with you, this is where you get centered and this is where you get lifted.

Strut your Stuff is a calling-out of sorts. It's a call to live the strongest life possible for you. Here, the word "strut" is about more than a glide or stride, here it's referenced as your personal stance, your genuine power. It's a call for your authoritative, true voice to come up, speak up, and refuse to give in. This is a coming-into-yourself book.

Life's experiences can strip away the initial love that was naturally implanted in us before we were born. Each time you have played yourself down, bit your tongue when you needed to defend or honor yourself, or denied your instinct- pieces of you chipped off here and there. Before long, these denials of self can result in our losing ourselves. We don't realize the damage immediately but it has a way of showing up in our relationships, our work, our ability to focus, and our health.

People have hurt you, they have disappointed you, taken you for granted, stolen from you, called you stupid, and you're afraid to trust again, afraid to love again, afraid to just "be" again. You've built a hard, rough surface around your heart, I know because I've been there. I know the pain of loosing oneself all to well but it is here, within these pages that I am asking you to consider softening that spot and reconnecting to your place of humbleness. Consider allowing meekness to override the turbulent conditions of the past.

I rediscovered my own strut after every material possession was stripped away, but your rediscovery may happen in a very different way. It doesn't take hitting rock bottom for everyone to regain that confident stride, sometimes all you need is a little adjustment a little tune-up. You also need to be aware that what's done is done, we can't turn back the hands of time and redo or retouch anything but we can use that stuff to fuel us in our new found quest.

I am a believer in a force much greater than me, I call it God and I won't even consider that God has brought me through all of the challenges I've faced and victories I've earned just to keep them to myself. I'm not afraid to say that I failed, or I lost, or I made foolish decisions. These are things that happened to me but these errors and mishaps don't define who I am. I am not my circumstances, and you are not the things that have happened to you.

I wrote this book for two reasons. First, I wanted to offer a reference guide for women to find or rediscover their power, for those who are back in the game or are ready to take things to another level. I wanted to create a space for women to make something grand move in their life—shake things up --step into their strut-- unapologetically. Second, I wrote it for myself. I still have times when I need to make sure I'm still on track, or when I need to get myself back into my own strut. I keep a close monitor on my thoughts and how I process information, and the work in these pages keep me in line with that. I also need to readapt my boundaries from time to time. I'm not the same woman I was ten years ago (thank goodness!), and as times change, my approach to self-monitoring needs to be refined and adjusted.

I have used and continue to use every single step in this book because they work. Through years of trial and error, pain and gain, success and failure-- I was able to pinpoint various strategies that necessitated results. I designed this guidebook based on what I've learned while studying spiritual enlightenment as it applies to everyday living. I've interviewed and studied under many terrific teachers whose ideas are ingrained in me in one way or another. I've been able to transform practical solutions into real life lessons and, through those, reconfirm my deepest commitment to myself.

When I made the decision to walk away from a blossoming career in television broadcasting, a lot of static erupted in my life and things took a fast turn toward a hellish darkness. I knew if I wanted to survive those hard times, I had to learn to manage myself instead of seeking temporary escapes in outside fixes. At one time or another, we all suffer but I don't want to see that desolation and hopelessness happen to any one. My greatest desire is to see each and every woman I encounter excel beyond what she believes is possible for her.

I've designed this book to be a resource. I wanted to create a go-to place for bringing power, purpose, and position back into your life. My intention is to supply information that can truly assist you wherever you are on your journey. Regardless of whether you're suspended between two worlds, trying to find yourself beneath the cooking and loads of laundry, or working on your next degree and need to up the ante, I'm hopeful that you will find something in each chapter that will enrich your life and guide you to meeting the most powerful and most important person in the world: YOU.

Through this book I hope that you will develop some strategies of your own and think for yourself as the information here pertains to you and your story. I hope that this experience will help you find or rediscover the most sacred part of you.

You won't get a Pollyanna approach here. Positive thinking and personal growth are important, but they will not somehow magically insulate the tough times from spilling over into your life. Problems will come, but when you have an assured plan of action and you know how to maximize your skills, you don't have to lose yourself in those difficult situations. A weak mind can't thrive during turbulent times. The work presented in this book is meant to help you ride on top of the waves and keep your mind strong with suggestions and strategies to help you handle adversity efficiently and intelligently. This book is meant to be a sidekick and reference manual for the strong sisters who always had it in them to be great. The information here is presented, and dedicated, to all the women who have fought and continue to fight against being less than their best, most honest selves.

When you see me at a conference or seminar, I hope you'll share with me how the steps in the following pages aided your strut and/or the lives of your loved ones. Maybe you'll email me and tell me about your boundaries and discoveries, I want to know that we're all growing and we're exceeding our wildest expectations.

Please write in this book. Seriously, write in this book. At the end of each chapter are Strutting Stones, which are think-tank stepping-stones to help you heighten your awareness. You'll find some diagrams, charts, and plenty of questions. Feel free to jot down your answers and ideas here or instead you may want to note your growth in a more spacious and personal place like a journal or notebook.

This book isn't intended to be read in one, two, or even three sittings. Take your time with it and go easy on yourself. I designed this book to give plenty of information for present and future use. You might connect with some points now and others might find their way to you next week, next month or next year. Don't worry about it, take what works for you and let the rest be.

Strut Your Stuff offers practical principles that you can insert into your life right now. Within these pages are many proven strategies that will add value to you life, for example--setting clear boundaries to prevent future disruptions and deviations from our path of responsible choices.

The book has two parts: Self ReView and Self ReNew. We can't renew ourselves without reviewing ourselves. So, the natural place to begin is at the beginning. By reviewing where you've been, you'll be able to understand how you arrived to the exact place you are today.

When you decide to make changes, a lot of people in your life won't follow you and that's OK. Don't let that hold you up for one minute. My desire is for you to continue referring to this book and internalizing the information on strengthening yourself so that nothing can rob you of the opportunity to thrive. As you read and study the principles I set forth in these pages, I believe that you will be enlightened, as I was, by ideals of putting yourself first and purposeful living. Afterall, this is all about you.

In the final pages I have produced a small list of Resources for you. These companies/organizations/associations are all geared toward empowerment. You might find a group that you will want to network with or an agency that can help out a friend. You may even find a cause that you will volunteer for. There are many great organizations in the world, this is just a short list of some that I wanted to share with you here.

Now...through all the research, studying, and sharing of setbacks and triumphs, I'm passing the strut torch to you, my friend, hoping that your light will become as brilliant as you suspect (and believe) that it can. I'm wishing for success for you, so that you can then lead others in your life to a genuine quality life that can't be bought or given to us, but which must be earned.

You'll find a lot of personal stories in these pages. I want you to get to know me as if we were sisters traveling on the same road. The fact that you are reading this book tells me that you know a thing or two about loss and discovery. You also know about the goodness of a higher power.

About that higher power--I have asked God to bless and guide us all as we work to contribute to a better, more peaceful world. I'm so honored that you are here with me.

Thank you for trusting me and for allowing me to share in your journey. I'm humbled by your willingness to strut alongside me and take away with you some of what experience and research have taught me. I don't have to know you to say that I admire and I respect you. I respect that we want the same things, and from that unfolds common experience of admiration. I want to see you win. I want you to clearly and totally understand that this world needs you to show up and live up to your ideals and goals. I want to see you strut.

~Raquel Eatmon

CAMERAS, CONFUSION, AND CLARITY

On the outside I seemingly had it all together, but on the inside I was toting a fractured spirit. There was a deep-rooted brokenness inside me that I mended with career moves, money, mindless consumption, and fake friends. Until one day, none of that worked—not even the occasional sleeping pill could quiet the conflict going on in my head. My attempts at seeking fulfillment in outside things came crashing down and I paid a very high price for it.

I worked hard at a career that most people might regard as

glamorous, high profile and exciting: I was a television news anchor and reporter. After learning the ropes of the business, I didn't find much honor or fulfillment in this career. I didn't have nor could I develop the passion for what some stations considered "news", nor did I support where the business was going, but I figured that since this was what I studied in college and it supported a great lifestyle, I was going to tough it out.

One day while preparing to anchor the five o'clock news, I was in the dressing room coaxing myself to put on a happy face. Tears bubbled up behind my big lashes and my anguished frown creased the orange lipstick that a supervisor told me he wanted me to wear. I started fanning my hands in front of my face, hoping to dry up the truth. I dabbed more powder on my face to conceal the damage and was confronted in the mirror with...me. I couldn't understand how I neglected to notice this before, I wondered just how much of myself had I abandoned while chasing this career that wasn't good for me. I got a real hard look at myself. I could see into my own eyes and the pain was enormous. I was tired of pretending of being something that I wasn't, tired of trying to please everyone else and swallow my own suffering, and sick of spending most of my time around people who didn't mean me well in any way.

Those tears soon transformed into pounding chest pains. Before I knew it, I walked into my manager's office and told him I had had enough. I was done.

After fulfilling my responsibilities to that job, I simply left the building. I walked away from a large income into, unforeseen to me at the time, what soon became near-poverty conditions.

My gutsy—or stupid—job move (however you choose to look at it) took a severe toll on my family, as a sudden recession was rolling our way. A few short months later, my husband's work was cut in half, we downsized from a 2100 square foot condo in the city to an 890 square foot apartment in a much less desirable area. We lost healthcare coverage and I could no longer afford the repairs for my paid-for dream car, so I had to let it go. And no pampering for this modern-day professional woman: hair services, manicures, pedicures, massages, and facials—all the beauty rituals I was accustomed to— were clearly in my past. But I lost something way more valuable than beauty treatments, cars, fancy apartments, or money: I lost myself. My courage dwindled, confidence fizzled, and my go-getter attitude seemed to have deserted me.

I lost pieces, no, chunks of myself through years of covering up emotions and hiding my truth. There was no pep in my step or glide in my stride. Instead, I was confronted with lots of confusion and disempowering self-criticism. I was disappointed in myself and very much disconnected from the woman I believed God wanted me to be. I questioned God, wondering where He was in all of this calamity. I was baffled over how I got into this mess in the first place.

I left a job that was enormously stressful and I left behind many disgruntled people, but I couldn't blame the job or former colleagues. I was angry with myself. I had made this bed and I had to lie in it. I ignored my instincts and disregarded previous danger signs (and believe me, there were plenty of warnings). I knew the type of work I wanted to do in television and I knew that most news agencies wouldn't buy into my idea, but I wanted to prove myself and show them what I could do. It didn't work and I didn't know exactly how to manage myself on what had turned into a wrong-track career, taking me away from the goals with which I started.

I knew that I wasn't the only woman who was in this predicament. I knew I wasn't the only woman who had used "stuff" to cover up internal emptiness. I knew there had to be others who were living a façade, faking happiness while a train wreck was happening on the inside. Yet most of the women in my circle didn't want to talk about such things, while others tried to justify artificial happiness that wasn't making them happy. That fact alone revealed a telling story of how so many of us have lost ourselves to work, family, food, or material possessions. We ignore the calling of our inner voice and that willful ignorance deadens us and removes us from our purpose in life.

The deeper I looked into the issue, the more I learned that there were a lot more women like me than I first realized. So many of us were tired of running in life, worn out from being what everyone else expected us to be. The more I talked to other women, I realized that most of us are not living our passion, we're not living on purpose, we're not really living—we're just breathing, numb to all the possibilities right before our eyes. So many ladies are ignoring their true calling and the next thing they know is a buildup of stress and pressure that spills over into medical emergencies like the dangerously high blood pressure which was one of the danger signs that I blithely ignored.

We're not bad people and we certainly aren't fools, we are only doing what we think is right for us at each moment. We are only coping with things the best way we know how; we're just trying to survive day-by-day.

I knew I didn't want to live that way again. I wanted to silence that voice in my head but I didn't know how. I certainly didn't understand the true meaning behind the motivational phrases quoted to me: "the power is within you," or "you are not your past or the things that happened to you." I needed to get to a better, healthier, more "me" place, but I had no idea where to begin. I knew that I hadn't managed my life well, but when I was in the thick of it, I thought I was OK because it all looked right from the outside—it was what society told me I was "supposed" to be doing. But the truth was that there was a tiny voice deep within me telling me that things were way off course. Even as I almost smothered that voice with the lifestyle I'd chosen, I knew that I wanted a better life...a stronger life. With that desire came many challenges. I knew that once I started to climb up that mountain toward the life I wanted, I would be tested and forced to stretch myself. I knew I had to make changes and a big initial change was becoming solemnly real with myself. I also knew that I had to put down the potato chips and red velvet cake and stare whatever void I was feeling right in the face.

In order to have order in my life I knew some of the truth I needed to face might seem brutal, unfair, even cruel, but I had to face it. I could either lie down and blame the world, keep blaming myself, or I could do something to change this situation which had become intolerable to my true self. I had only a sliver of determination left, and some days I didn't even have that. I started this fearsome climb with a simple prayer: "God, stay close to me."

After walking out of that last job, A few months later, a friend of my mother's walked back into my life. It had been years since I saw Diane and we had never been much more than cordial with one another, but this time was different. She saw right through me, and she said, "You are right where you need to be." She told me that, while I felt like I had lost everything and life was crashing in, there was actually a beautiful thing starting to happen inside of me. She warned me that it would take as much time as I needed to "get it," she assured me that the answers would come as long as I stayed open to receiving them.

On all counts, Diane was right.

My often-unconscious choice to be inauthentic with myself sent me on a journey that blew my mind. It was a bumpy road ahead but I was right where I needed to be. When Diane gave me that preview of the road ahead, I was at a crossroads between where I started and where I could be. While the struggle to achieve my possibilities would be challenging, I would later find that the very struggle I feared had great rewards to offer me.

In that initial space of both solitude and chaos—my "rock bottom"—I couldn't help but think of other women who hit tough times and survived them. I thought about some women who had it a lot worse than me and how they, too, climbed out and turned their stories around. I had no idea that my comeback would be such a compelling process. I would berate myself repeatedly before learning to love and forgive myself, I would revisit childhood pain before becoming a woman of action, and I would learn how to heal myself.

I came from humble beginnings so I knew about living on a financial minimum, but still the sting of losing so much that I'd built up was very personal and poignant. My professional accolades were my own achievement. No one forced me to follow that career path, I paid my full share of dues to advance and I worked hard for every bit of my professional success. I was also responsible for every single decision I made. Each one of the choices I made turned out to be a promise in my pain as it all has led me to the very moment, right here with you.

GOING TO WORK...

I don't want another woman to experience this wasteful, draining, and heart wrenching cycle. I don't want another woman to lose herself to worldly possessions or to become anyone's doormat, it's not necessary. I certainly don't want anyone to be thrown from her glory- that is, get stuck in her strut. I didn't want to stand by and watch another woman lose belief or faith in her ability to rise above it. I took the lessons of the past to strengthen me in the present. I began extensive research and contemplation on my own upbringing and life choices. I was seeking to understand not what was wrong with me but what was right with me. I wanted to know what was preventing me from having a successful life while being true to my self. I knew that it was possible to have a fulfilling career, meaningful relationships, and monetary success along with a positive and healthy relationship with one's self—I've seen others accomplish it.

Ripping through layers of baggage, I discovered streams of self-sabotage, betrayal, fear of success, and unworthy feelings. I began to unravel the reasons why I felt so isolated, and I tapped into the very moment when I stopped standing up for myself and when I stopped cheering for that little girl still living inside of me.

This all came with work...a lot of work. I surrounded myself with information and enrolled in several intense multi-day forums, I threw myself into leadership courses, discussion groups, and personal and professional growth seminars and webinar series. I sought out women who I admired and began spending time with them. I invested time in reading, studying, and making a concerted decision to practice and apply what I'd learned to my own life. I went back to a place of love and examined the relationships in my life, I closed the friendships that didn't serve me well and opened up new ones that supported my new view.

I also meticulously examined my decision to go into broadcasting, as well as my decision to leave that profession. When I started working in broadcasting, it was my desire to get a foot in the door, make a name for myself, and then earn my way to developing a franchise (a specialty weekly segment on a topic like Women Who Rock, How to Run Yourself Like a Business, Health & Relationships, or the like). I had dreams of someday working on a national magazine or morning show highlighting ways of living better and smarter. I thought that local news was a perfect place to hone my writing and interviewing skills and learn the business and I guess in a way it did hone a very different type of skill. It did teach me a lot about life and how crucial it is to live with passion and purpose and never give up on oneself. Still, I questioned why is it that some of us have to endure so much pain to learn the lessons and advance to a quality life with measurable peace and joyfulness? The answer to that question circles back around to the advice of my dear friend Diane: we get it when we get it, we don't, however, get to choose how we learn what we need to learn, the important fact is that we learn how to cope and how to strategize for the things we want.

SOFTENING HARDENED FEELINGS

I thought walking away from a well-paying job and hitting hard times was the end of my downward spiral, but it turned out to be only a first step on a journey back to myself. Hidden behind all of my apparent success was a woman who didn't know how to run herself like a business. She— I —hadn't mastered the skills to build strong boundaries and step into authentic power (for me, authentic power is leading life from my most sacred, pure and true self over worldly perceptions and beliefs). Underneath it all was someone who was still too damaged from past hurts to make progress on herself.

We are hardened by our past difficulties and holding on to these imprisons us. This memory of hardship prevents us from accepting the gifts of the present moment. I had to adapt to a new way of releasing the humiliation and embarrassment of growing up in a house where

I witnessed harsh words and even acts of violence by and toward family members.

My mother was just sixteen years old when she gave birth to me, I had to learn to let go of what she could or couldn't give me because in all actuality, this woman did the absolute best she could under the circumstances she was in. I also learned to forgive those who tried to manipulate me into doing dishonest or conniving work. I had to excuse those who told me that I wouldn't amount to much nor would I have "good luck," (especially after understanding that there was no such thing as luck—just opportunity and possibility tripled with preparedness).

Once I took a real, hard look at how old wounds of the past were affecting me in my adult life, I knew I had to let it all go, forgive each and every person for any harm they brought on me. I also had some work to do in the self-forgiveness department.

When we let things fester and build up in us, it creates a rottening blockage that prevents all sorts of possibilities and opportunities to flow our way. Working through this single principle of forgiveness brought about big changes in my life. I connected the dots with family and old associates, understanding that people are only doing what was passed down to them. I had to stop making my family wrong or bad in my mind and just see them for the people that they are. I had to focus on the love they showed me. As rough or tough as my childhood seemed, I did receive love, and plenty of it. My family loved me the best way they knew how and for that I am extraordinarily grateful.

PRIORITIZING

I was working the three a.m. shift and we got a call that a

woman had been thrown from a speeding car and was believed to be dead. My photographer and I jumped in the live truck and rushed to the scene. Driving up that dark road, I noticed a human figure in the street under a dull streetlight. The person's arms were stretched toward the sky, in a fighting motion. It was indeed a woman, with long black hair. She seemed to be peering upward, her blank eyes staring from a cigarette-burned face. Her pants were wadded around her ankles, and the recent char marks on her skin showed that someone—perhaps the monstrous people who dumped her in this desolate spot—had tried to set her on fire. It was dreadful and I had to go stand in front of a television camera and go live on this story in a matter of minutes. We didn't have her name or any information about what was happening. Police were still arriving on the scene and I felt sick from the inhumanity on view in front of me.

I didn't think people wanted to wake up to this horrible scene on their morning news, but I tried to put myself in the frame of mind that maybe someone in that area saw something and could help bring in the killer. I focused on the victim as a woman and the angle that there may be relatives or children who are wondering where she is or when she is coming home.

I was told by my producer to stay on the scene for the rest of my shift and continue giving updates. I was preparing to do that, but about forty minutes later, I got a call from the producer telling me that my photographer and I should shut down at the scene and head back toward the newsroom until we receive a lead for another story. I told my producer that the police were still canvassing the area, and giving me information as it becomes available, but her response was, "I just got a call and this woman was a drug addict and prostitute, no one cares about that stuff."

I knew that my producer meant this wasn't an "important" story in comparison to a soccer mom found dead in the suburbs, however, I felt differently. I understood the nature of the news business, but I couldn't deny myself my own truth that this woman meant something to someone. I felt like I had something in common with that woman. She was a human being who may have made mistakes but was just as deserving of attention as the next woman. Apparently I was wrong. I was pulled from the story, and I never learned the woman's name; her killer, as far as I know, was never caught.

I had seen enough suffering growing up, I didn't need to keep reminding myself of the painful evil in life on a daily basis.

I also didn't find it very helpful to knock on a rap victims door or ask a mother to talk on camera after her child was murdered. These things came with the job but didn't align with my spirit. There are still lessons in those out of alignment jobs, relationships or daily experiences. Sometimes the things we need to learn come shinning through in the most unsuspecting ways.

When I looked back on my career to date in broadcasting and how I often unconsciously allowed it to change me, I learned a great deal about who I am and who I want to become. I am glad that I had a chance to walk away when I began to compromise my values and lose myself. I risked a lot in leaving, though what I didn't know at the time was that I would find so much more by leaving.

Armed with new knowledge, I began to strategize a plan of action for getting out of the hole that I'd unknowingly been responsible for digging. I found that most of the turmoil and suffering of the past could've been avoided if I had known how to manage things differently.

Once the system started working for me and I took my cycle in a more positive direction, I extended my plan and insights toward giving to other women. I felt so rewarded by this new way of conducting my life with honesty and responsibility that I began hosting women's weekend retreats at my mother's home. I wanted to share what I was discovering and open up a comfortable space for other women to talk and grow.

I proposed and started writing a weekly lifestyle newspaper column, "Be Inspired with Raquel" (Gannett News). For more than five years, I have searched for the extraordinary in ordinary living, hoping to encourage my readers to reach for new ways to make an impact in the world.

After leaving the TV news business, I began to combine all of the data, facts and details of my life and my self, I realized that we are all more alike than we are different. We're all seeking wholeness and to lead a life that has meaning. A lot of people may not understand the ups and downs of working in the media industry but we all can identify with fulfilling our purpose or working toward it. We all can identify with feelings of hurt, grief, and pain; we all want to be loved and celebrated. When I really understood that, I found that a part of my life's purpose was to be a catalyst in this work for others. I teamed up with a professional/ personal development company and got certified to lead public seminars for people in the workforce. From there, I started designing my own programs and presenting them to corporations and organizations, as well as providing lifestyle coaching for individuals. I enjoyed the work so much that I started my own company and worked hard to understand entrepreneurship and how to earn a living doing what I love.

MANAGING ME

We are trained on the basics. We know how to do our jobs

because we're trained; we can run the machines and operate heavy equipment because someone has shown us how to do it.

If you are an entrepreneur, you have access to many workshops and conferences on how to run your business. As kids, most of us were taught how to do chores, so we grew up knowing how to care for a home with cooking and cleaning, lawn-mowing and leaf-raking. If you lead a team of employees at work, you've probably attended team-building and leadership events on how to effectively manage your staff. We have a huge vocabulary of basic life skills training, but we're not often trained on how to manage ourselves. This is the one skill that we must develop on our own, if at all, and it's the one skill that not only allows us to be at peace with ourselves but also positions us to soar beyond our wildest dreams and desires. Mastering this skill opens us up to unlimited resources, yet most people don't even know, let alone believe, that it's possible.

Learning to manage myself was a turning point in my life that changed me forever. Out of that change, my Woman of Power conference was born, as well as many other events that speak to proactive women who are in search of their own personal greatness. My passion for partnering with others supports my own story of stepping into my Strut. I am so very grateful for every single right turn, wrong turn, U-turn and detour that I made, all of those moves helped me define my purpose and you can only appreciate how satisfying it is to find your purpose if you have ever lived without it.

Part One
Self ReView

1

WHERE'S MY STUFF?

There is a silent, free-flowing giant in us all and when you are in line with that gentle gracefulness, you can never truly lose your magnificence.

It was my first year in college. I'd left my native Buckeye State (Ohio) for the friendliness of the beachy side of Virginia. While I was studying communications in Norfolk, a very kind and generous professor took a liking to me. He took me under his wing and told me that he saw something special in the way I communicated during class. He put me on a mock television set, threw some scripts at me, and began working with me, teaching me how to hone my talent as a future broadcaster. Professor James went a step more than even these very helpful exercises--he arranged a luncheon for me to meet one of the top male T.V. news anchors in the area. Unbeknownst to the Professor, I had a bit of a crush on this anchor.

So there we were in a great restaurant: me, face-to-face with my idol/crush, and Professor James talking up my currently raw but surely someday great talent for broadcasting. I sat quietly, trying to hide the fact that I, a broke, starving college student, hadn't seen a meal like this for months. Trying not to make a bad impression on this illustrious (and good-looking!) potential networking contact, I took small bites... lots of them...quickly...and then, out of nowhere, it happened. I let out the loudest burp imaginable. It seemingly came from someplace I wasn't familiar with (perhaps a deep, formerly undiscovered pit in my belly) and it lasted for at least four seconds! It interrupted the Professor's cheerful banter and got the attention--though not in the way I wanted--of my anchorman crush.

The anchor's mouth dropped open and he said, "Wow, what a big sound from such a small girl." I wilted inside and tried to contain my embarrassed grimace realizing first, that this guy still saw me as a "little girl", so marrying him was out of the picture and second, he'd always think of me as the little girl with a huge belch.

As soon as the Professor dropped me off at my dorm, I ran into the room, lay on the floor, and laughed myself silly. I laughed until I cried. My roommates could barely get the story out of me because I was hysterically letting out the giggles that I'd managed to clamp down until lunch was over.

What happened to that girl? The girl that laughed at life's hiccups--or in this case, burps? I would somehow become disenchanted with her through a combination of cruel experiments and missed opportunities at self-loyalty.

It would be years, even decades before I'd meet up with that carefree girl again. I had to do some digging for her. I had to rummage through piles of personal scolding and worldly afflictions but, like a mummy in the tomb, she was still there, still laughing at herself and unbothered by what (most) others thought of her.

THE UNVEILING

I have learned that we can cripple ourselves without even realizing we're doing it. Many people have been deadened by various experiences and they are emotionally unavailable when it comes to living fully and completely. It's not that they're bad people, they're just living through a situation where they believe their hardships are a direct correlation to their worth or are a symbol of who they are. They define themselves by what they have or don't have, what they did or didn't do. They beat themselves up and it changes them, they lose their luster and decline from living a life of truth. We must learn how to accept what was and not allow it to dictate who we are in the now. We've got to sharpen our skills and snatch back any pieces of self we may have lost or given away through past situations. We must master a system that empowers our supreme ability to rule by faith and action over fear and negligence.

This is where you start cracking open the vault of the past. This is where you get nice and familiar with the little and big things you've been avoiding, hiding, or trying to escape. The faster you can make a commitment to go through this painful but necessary process, the faster things will move forward for you.

First things first, it's OK to let go of the stuff you're hiding. No one is watching; you're not on live television or publishing your private thoughts in a book or magazine. Here's a secret that you might not know: most people are pretending at something. So many of us hide behind big hair, big sunglasses, and big personalities. We cultivate conceitedness to cover up feelings of unworthiness. We hide behind a plastered-on smile to hide our shame from days gone by. It's OK--it's called "being human", but most of us think we're the only ones that have to go through these charades.

Isn't it funny how we see people who seemingly have it all together and we automatically assume they're doing great? We see their sharp, trendy haircut, their perfectly rouged cheeks, a glammed-up wardrobe and new set of wheels, but we have no idea what their internal dialogue is, or if they berate themselves or even really like themselves. We don't have a clue if a person we see is battling heart disease, or trying to escape a bad marriage, or once like my own former self, stressing herself into a 210/110 blood pressure health emergency. We don't know the hurts that lie behind another woman's cute pleasant-looking smile. We don't know the troubles in her heart, we only know what we see on the surface, and if all looks OK then we figure that all must be OK.

We lose our power to many things, but what continues to amaze me is how much we allow our past to dictate our present moments. That 210/110 blood pressure was mine and it was also where I started discovering how I was pulling pieces of the past into present moment living. I was sabotaging myself without even knowing it.

220/110

It was on a warm though tolerable July day. I woke up and went for a short jog, came home and ate a bowl of steel cut oatmeal, finishing with some whole grain toast and a cup of my favorite green tea. The day was clearly off to a trouble-free start.

Later that afternoon I decided to tend to some much-needed landscaping chores in our backyard. I don't exactly have a green thumb, but the basic tasks on that day's list were within my few gardening skills. Since my husband and I had just purchased a new home, I felt a sense of pride de-weeding our new, hard-earned space.

There was one plant, a real stubborn one that was so heavily rooted I had to get a shovel for the job. I got to digging only to find more roots, tied in knots, closely attached to the others. I started to see that this weed was more deeply embedded than I first realized. I stood on the shovel, even jumped on it a few times hoping to penetrate those gnarled roots.

About fifteen minutes into my battle with this plant, I totally related to its roots and all the "stuff" knotted up beneath the surface, just like old thoughts or stories we've been telling ourselves. It's so hard to dig this stuff up to the surface, deal with it, and get it out of the way, making way for more beautiful things to be planted. It's challenging to get to the source. I've often heard of gardening to be therapeutic but my thoughts as I battled this behemoth took me to a whole new level of introspection.

The project became personal. With each dig or pull, a metaphoric meaning blossomed. It all translated to my life! Even through all of the previous personal growth I had achieved, I still hadn't managed or dealt with some things. My thoughts turned to a longstanding family matter as my hands were busy with yardwork. Two hours later my job was complete. I felt some release as I worked to put my emotions into some sort of perspective but yet again, I felt a slight sensation of indecision. Something was still bothering me, but I couldn't put my finger on it, I took the thoughts to bed with me that evening.

The next day, my husband, Dexter, and I had dinner with friends at a cozy restaurant. I normally enjoy a glass of wine with dinners out, but for some reason I passed on it that night. Near the end of the meal, I felt light-headed, as if I were going to faint. In my mind, I could just see a terrifying scene of how that would look and how embarrassed I'd feel, passing out in the quaint restaurant, so I plastered on a smiling face to keep my lady-like demeanor. As we walked to the car, this uncomfortable feeling got stronger. I asked Dexter to drive me to the nearest pharmacy so I could check my blood pressure which we both thought was a weird request seeing that I've always had an ordinary, healthy reading of 120/80. I had a feeling, though, that something just wasn't right.

At the drug store's automatic blood pressure machine, my reading was a little high. I sat down, practiced some deep breathing techniques, and rechecked myself. The numbers were going up instead of down, despite my attempts to calm myself. I dreaded going to the hospital, mainly because we didn't have healthcare coverage at that time, and on top of that, I've always prided myself on exercising and taking care of myself, I did not want to admit that my health could be in danger.

Dexter insisted we go to the nearest emergency room--apparently something about my condition had him worried, too. En route to the hospital, I arrived at the decision that, no matter how much the bill would be, my health was worth it, I was worth it. I recognized that potential medical bills were not more important than keeping myself healthy. And I was definitely not feeling healthy as we hurried to the ER.

Once we arrived there, a very pleasant paramedic wrapped the cuff around my arm. As I was bantering with him, we were both shocked to see the display on the device read a very worrisome 220/110--close to twice my usual blood pressure stats. The paramedic turned to all business, jumped up, and quickly alerted the doctor.

Five hours, several tests, and plenty of medication later--nothing. The ER staff found nothing, not one thing wrong other than this alarming, and for me annoying, surge in blood pressure. Nothing on the MRI, CAT scan, X-ray, vitals--everything was great, with no reason for this mysterious episode. I could only connect it to the previous afternoon's weed pulling which involved some emotional upset. I believe the stress from that impromptu "therapy" session got to me, and the doctor agreed that stress can cause a flareup, but she noted it's not often that stress alone causes such a huge spike from a usually normal pressure.

My numbers went back to normal shortly after that frightening night, and they have remained at my usual levels without medication. There has still been no medical explanation for why that scare happened, but I truly believe that when we don't deal with our stuff and get to the "root" of it, figuratively speaking, it gets lodged in us and causes all sorts of severe ramifications to our health and soul.

BEING HUMAN

For me, on that day my warning sign came by way of a medical alert. For you, it might be getting fired from a job, being unable to communicate effectively with others, weathering a painful divorce, or lugging around years of anger toward a parent or sibling.

The warning sign or wakeup call is different for all of us but the shame, anger, guilt, frustration, and other emotions stuck in us eat away at the core of who we really are, just the same. Some people will leave this earth never unfolding the hidden pains in family secrets.

They will die with that bitterness, leaving the undiscovered sweetness hidden beneath a mountain of sorrow. They die with it all locked up inside of them.

The very fact that you are reading this book relays pertinent information. It says that you are committed to growing yourself and identifying your personal best, and that you are determined to live a strong life. Because you are scanning these pages, it also says that--like me--somewhere things got off track for you. Somehow some great content in your life got misconstrued, mismanaged, and misplaced. This disconnection from ourselves doesn't make us stupid, dumb, or even foolish, it just makes us human and if you believe in a higher power--something bigger than you--then you'll understand when I say that human beings are created by a powerful source. Your Creator doesn't make anything stupid, dumb, or foolish, but we fall prey to these negative thought patterns through unhealthy habits of berating ourselves or even, in some cases, considering ourselves more worthy than others.

This odd condition of being human is simply stated, but often is confusing to understand and difficult to accept. It's challenging to give ourselves a pass when we mess up or seemingly ruin a situation or opportunity. However, if we could only accept and internalize the fact that we don't know what we don't know and we do the best with what we do know, then we could relax a bit and go easier on ourselves.

There are many places we humans can lose our strut. We all have several familiar dumping grounds and I want to draw your attention to four of the most common places we lose our steam and our strut: Put-Downs, Over-Apologizing, the Need to Please, and the Doormat.

THE PUT-DOWNS

As if the rude people of the world don't beat us up enough, here we come with our own treacherous words, hard grievances, and mad hearts and we direct all this poison at ourselves. We rant and rave about what we should've said, could've done, or wished we hadn't said. We're so strong-minded that we can rehash an event that happened fifteen years ago and fool our body and mind into the feeling that we're right there in that moment again.

International spiritual leader and best-selling author Deepak Chopra explains in his book "Ageless Mind, Timeless Body" how closely in sync the mind and body are. He shared medical proof that the mind narrates a story and the body just reacts to it. Even if it's an old--or even imagined--story, the body reacts accordingly.

If Dr. Chopra is right--and, based on my blood pressure reading, I believe he is--we compromise our present moment living by sifting through old rubbish from the previous years. Often, it's like we're reliving the experience in our minds, and, before you know it, your heart is racing again, the same as it did when the event actually happened. Your breathing deepens and a scowl is plastered across your forehead. These visual signs doesn't compare to what's happening on the inside of the body.

When we self-loathe, we are abandoning ourselves and pricking away at the most valuable thing we have--our self-esteem. If you really want to generate energy, try redirecting your thoughts. You can relive an empowering moment just as you can relive a disempowering one. You can go to a good memory of a time when you felt alive and full of passion, take that into a meditation, and allow those great feelings to surface and blot out the negative ones. I'll dive deeper into how to do this in Chapter 2.

We have great expectations of ourselves, and there is nothing wrong with that. We should be ambitious and goal-oriented, but we must also make allowances for our errors and mis-steps.

Dwelling on past failures doesn't serve us well. Living with that negativity in mind prevents us from diving into our personal power and embracing authenticity. We also lose touch with personal relationships because we're stuck back in time, while the current relationship is happening in the now. You can't be both stuck in the past and living in the now at the same time. You will be in one place or the other, but you must choose.

Take a step back and be willing see those little past blunders as something different. If you were training a five-year-old to ride a bicycle and she fell a few times, you wouldn't berate her and constantly remind her of the falls as she struggled to succeed, would you? Then why do the same thing to yourself? Go back to your own five- or six-year-old self, see those pigtails or freckles and look into those eyes of wonderment. You can't convince me that the little girl at your core deserves to be punished, humiliated, and reminded of past mistakes.

As you move through this stage of your strut, use your inner child as a reminder to relax on the self-loathing. That voice may have popped up already, trying to drive home a point: "yeah, but we're adults now, we are supposed to know better." Where can we get a handbook "knowing better by age thirty?" There isn't one. We're all marching to a different beat. What one woman learned at 17 another one learned at 71? In Strutville, we don't have time lines or deadlines for becoming whole; we just pick up a map, choose a route, and start walking in that new direction at our own pace.

I'M NOT SORRY...FOR EVERYTHING

The words "I'm sorry" are so delicate and revealing. They help us relay empathy, and they can quickly touch the heart of another person. "I'm sorry you're faced with such a hard time right now." "I'm sorry for what I said last night, I'd like to explain my position." Those sentiments beautifully demonstrate the heartfelt meaning attached to the sympathetic message. Being sorry for being who you are, though, doesn't have the same meaning.

A 2010 research study in Psychological Study Journal found that women do indeed apologize more than men. Researchers point out that women reported committing more offensive acts than their male counterparts but what are we really apologizing for?

If you listen closely, I believe you'll begin to take notice of your colleagues apologizing for talking too low, too fast, too much...or they'll apologize for not talking at all. Beyond admitting to wrongdoing, some of us apologize for the basics of things, from laughing "too much" to having a string of spinach caught on a front tooth. It's amazing how often and how much some women say, "I'm sorry."

Maybe some of this excessive apology is unconscious, or maybe it's taught by our mothers who wanted us to be polite little ladies. You can be nice, without overindulgence in unnecessary guilt.

Words have power because we give meaning to the words. Repeating, "I'm sorry" for weeks upon weeks, months upon months, year after year clearly creates a pattern. Before you know it, you have embellished a theme: I am sorry. For some people that translates into a belief system that says, they are in fact, sorry. Not in an apologetic way, but in a pathetic way. Labeling yourself as a "sorry" person is one of those little things we do to ourselves that snuffs out our power and silences our strong voices.

The next time your tongue rolls toward "I'm sorry", ask yourself, "what am I sorry for, and is a sincere apology needed here?" Try replacing a routine "I'm sorry" with a more explained response: "I understand this happened to you, please let me know if I can help you get through this situation." A simple "excuse me" is also appropriate in most cases. Drop the unneeded sorrys--you've apologized for quite enough already.

THE NEED TO PLEASE

It's been implanted in us since childhood, a desire to plaster a wide smile across the face of our over-achieving mother or a hope to brighten the spirits of our favorite aunt, who never seemed quite happy. As youngsters, we needed our fathers to pick us up and plant a loving kiss on the cheek with a reassuring, "that's my girl" remark. We wanted to make others proud of us and when we did, the general consensus was so pleasantly appealing that we wanted to do it again and again.

Somewhere in between childhood pleasantries and adult disorder, many women neglected to cut the needy cord of approval. They never learned how to stop seeking approval of others to nurture fulfillment within. Women like this burn themselves out trying to please everyone else.

You might fear your friend getting upset with you if you don't help her. You might fear a partner leaving you if you don't give him what he wants. You feel as though you'll be passed over again for a promotion if you don't say yes to all the overtime and take-home work that no one else is doing. These are chronic set ups for a bigger and perhaps more recognizable issue. Needing to please is directly related to our feelings of self-worth and self-value. Somewhere underneath all of that overstepping, people are feeling unworthy. Even with good looks, great talents, and amazing abilities, we can still be in the dark about our own worth.

If you could identify and embrace your most prized possession, there would be no worry about what others thought of you based on your actions or acts of kindness toward them.

We walk around in a fog of funk and frustration, trying to figure out what everyone else wants and we try like hell to give them what they need as our own personal well dry up and shrinks away. We suffer through hallow relationships and broken marriages because we've placed the other person's needs above our own.

You will never be able to fulfill the expectations of others. The moment you succeed at one thing, they'll send you another one, one that's bigger, bolder, and perhaps more dangerous than the previous.

It was important to win over the approval of our parents and grandparents as we learned about love and achievement at a young age. As children we developed ideas about what was considered to be a good job and how we could do the task better next time. We searched for feedback through the faces of our elders. That was then, this is now. You and I are not here to try to win approval from others. You can scale back from being a "yes" woman and agree to becoming a gracious "no" woman when appropriate. You can begin this journey at a very straightforward place with a simple question: is this something I want to do? Outside of the random acts of kindness, compromises, and sacrifices we all make on occasion, dig deep to find the meaning of your actions and what--if any--pleasure you are getting from the overflowing and overextension of "yes, yes, yes".

THE DOORMAT

I remember the day the news broke about a well-known football player who allegedly tried to kill himself using painkillers. It was a big story, and even the national news was weighing in. Every reporter in town was trying to get to someone who knew the athlete and find out what happened and why.

It was a media frenzy and at the time, I was the only one in our newsroom who had a direct connection with the player, via his personal trainer. Many of the top reporters didn't have a source close to the athlete who was willing to talk to them.

When I mentioned that I contacted the trainer and that he was interested in talking to me with his desire to defend the ballplayer, everyone fell silent. I believed they were actually shocked that I could muster up such a resourceful interview for this big story.

After some of the producers met and decided on the angle that our station would take for this story, we later regrouped and the producers had some news of their own to share with me.

I walked into our afternoon meeting and told the producer that we had the interview--the personal trainer was out of state but was willing to talk to us if we went to see him. One of the managers quickly spoke up and said that he would like to fly a crew out to do the interview. This manager mentioned other reporters for his team, but not me.

Just like that, this manager was willing to take my effort and give it to someone else. I sat there, stunned at first, and I didn't say a thing. I said nothing because I had stopped caring. I knew this manager didn't respect me as a journalist or as a person. I was tired of defending myself.

I sat there in that meeting numb, and suddenly another manager spoke up and said, "why would we send another reporter to interview the personal trainer when he's Raquel's contact?"

"Exactly!" I thought, "why didn't I say that?" That man's voice woke me up out of my I-don't-care haze and I realized that my inability to speak up for myself and my habit of allowing others to push me around was nauseating.

In the end, I got the interview and a very big lesson. Regardless of my feelings about the local news business and how I stopped caring for various parts of it, I surely wasn't going to stop caring for myself. I had betrayed myself far too long and it was causing a lot of damage. My choice to let some things go was costing me more than loss of respect from colleagues.

What happens to doormats? People step on them again and again. I had given people permission to mistreat me and disregard me--to step all over me--but that little episode was my breaking point.

Months later, that same manager who wanted to replace me on my own story for the football player came back with another odd request. He was in another newsroom, thirty miles away from my newsroom, and through a conference call he asked me to travel over to his area to cover a story. This wasn't an unreasonable request as all of the reporters covered both newsrooms from time to time.

There were other people listening in on this particular call, I explained that I would need to use a station vehicle, as my car was in the shop. All the station cars and live trucks were out on other assignments, so the manager told me to take a bus. He was, in fact, asking me to carry out a work errand on public transportation, which--as far as I know--no other reporter had ever been asked to do, the station always found a way to get the reporter to the scene of a story.

I don't have any problem with riding buses, but I believe that my employer should be responsible for transporting me to and from work assignments--this was the normal routine for all of the other on-air personalities at that station. I took this suggestion as a slap in the face--a true reflection of how he felt about me, but, more importantly, this was a huge telltale sign of how I allowed this manager and others to treat me. I decided at that moment that I wasn't willing to compromise myself any more.

I excused myself from the room, still half-shocked by the request, and I called this manager's boss. I told the boss that I was humiliated by the manager's request and that I deserved more respect than I had been given. That conversation went on for several minutes and, twenty minutes later another manager was driving me to the other site, after having gotten a sincere apology from the manager who suggested the bus ride.

The next day I came into work and some of my very humorous colleagues obviously heard about what happened. My desk was festooned with little sponge model buses--giveaways from the local transit system. I laughed out loud when I saw this unusual salute to my tenacity, and gave myself a pat on the back and a friendly "that-a-girl!"

WHAT'S IT COSTING YOU?

When our strut is stuck we are losing. We are losing ourselves. We are losing our place in the world, the workplace, the community, and our homes. That loss translates to your children. They might hear the lesson you're trying to teach, but it's your actions that they will emulate. It's the passion in your eyes, the victory in your voice, and the pep in your step that they truly identify with.

When your power has been zapped, your greatness is deflated.

You wither to a commonality that wasn't intended for you. The confidence meter swings off the low end of the dial. Your health might bear the burden of your low self-esteem. You miss the many opportunities to grow as woman, as a leader, and as a spiritual being. You undermine yourself by not learning what's in store for you. The straightness in your back slumps away, your handshake weakens, your clairvoyant voice cracks, and your eye contact turns into no contact.

Before I clearly understood my personal power, hitting hard times meant, to me, some sort of diminishment. I lost something; I lost that glisten in my eye, the ability to think on my feet, and I lost a thousand little other little things that added up to the bigness of me. When I committed to knowing and loving myself, no matter what, I was able to deal much more efficiently with setbacks and life's other problems. There is a silent, free-flowing giant in us all and when you are in line with that gentle gracefulness, you can never truly lose your magnificence.

MYSTERY AND TIME

You are right where you need to be. Whatever led you to this quiet moment of reflection in your bedroom or some time for yourself amid the busyness of a subway, you're now perfectly positioned for what's next for you.

People who know me well will tell you that I'm not a believer in coincidences. I do, however, believe that there is order in all of our lives. No matter how calm or chaotic things are, there is still order. This order comes as a result of the experiences we've encountered, and is led by the choices we've made. Other than in violent situations, you are right where you need to be in accordance to your life's calling.

Even if you feel like I did, completely off track, you're where you need to be. Think about all of the things and events and right turns, left turns, u-turns, and detours you've made--that path has all landed you right here, right now for a reason.

Stop guessing, stop pushing yourself in a hurry trying to figure it all out. The answers will come. I was conducting a lifestyle power coaching session with a woman in her early thirties and this was our first session. Right out of the gate, she asked me how long it would take her to forgive her cheating ex-husband, confront her unloving mother, and forgive herself for loathing. I asked her how long it took her to accumulate all of this "stuff". She didn't have an answer for me. I tried to help her understand that it takes time to undo what's been done. It took time to get here and it's going to take time to get "there", wherever "there" is for you. You need to be open to and have a willingness to review old stories and cycles and to rewrite your truth onto it. You are separating from your past and from the thinking you currently hold, now it's just a matter of helping you understand that.

✤ STRUTTING STONES ✤

1. Review the four sections (Put Downs, Over-Apologizing, the Need to Please, and the Doormat). In a journal or notebook, jot down where you see pieces of yourself in these categories. You may see that you have actions and experiences evenly distributed in each category, or you might find 80% in one and only 20% in all of the others. Try to remember specific events when you've given in to one or more of these categories.

2. What has this experience in putting yourself down cost you?

3. Regarding issues surrounding self-worth, what would it take for you to feel truly worthy of all of the relationships in your life, if you could let go of the need to please or always putting others before yourself?

4. Attempt to monitor the need to please. When faced with a request or asked to do a favor, ask yourself, "is this something I really want to do or am I just trying to please the other person?" If you're only doing it to please someone else, step back away from the situation and reevaluate your position. If appropriate, make a point of kindly denying the request.

2

RESONANT REFLECTION

"The past is never where you think you left it." ~ *Katherine Anne Porter*

I was undressing in the gloomy girls' locker room with its distinctive odor--a mixture of cleaning fluid and old sour pickle juice. I was staring down at the mandatory blue and white gym uniform that my mother could barely afford. Growing up, my family never had a lot of money but my mother made ends meet and, with the help of her boyfriend Terry, I was able to attend a private Catholic school for grades 1-8. I despised the school because I was one of only a handful of black kids there. And that difference stood out this day in the locker room more than any other day.

As I pulled off my green and blue plaid jumper and unbuttoned the cotton white shirt and slid it down my back. I heard a sneer from a blond-haired white girl. With a pointed stare at me, she hissed to the rest of her popular friends, "ewwww, she looks dirty." Those cronies of hers snickered along with her cruel evaluation of me. I looked down at my caramel-colored skin covering my bony shoulders. The light skin color that brought me ridicule from the darker-skinned black girls in my neighborhood was now also prompting mean comments from my creamy white classmates. I didn't say a word. I didn't defend myself, I didn't cry, and I didn't run home to tell my mother. I swallowed my misery at being the target for my bullying peers. Another invisible mark on my self-esteem and a burning strike on my spirit. I did not know there would be plenty more of those little cruelties to come, maybe not remarks about my skin color but digs about my big forehead, my big feet, and my broken family. This first remark bit hard into my psyche and made me feel like I was somehow less worthy than those other girls.

I took that incident from my 8-year-old self and unknowingly carried it all through my twenties and into my thirties. I was hauling an insurmountable amount of baggage that boiled down to two judgments of me: "I don't belong", and "I'm not good enough"-- which deals directly with self-worth. Little did I know that I was pulling this childish misrepresentation into adulthood and through that experience, I was making decisions for my career and household. That old paradigm was a pattern and very often, I was thinking through that scratched and blurry lens. So no matter how put-together I seemed in my television broadcasts or how articulate I sounded during a speech, I still felt the weight of those staring, accusing eyes and hateful comments from my early years.

So how did my mind interpret those feelings of misfitting and not being good enough? In my head, I'm still just an 8-year-old little girl learning to cope on her own. I could have developed anger issues, becoming sullen and hostile; I could have lashed out and punched the girl in the locker room. Internalizing this hurt was just my way of dealing with a situation that pained me when I was 8. And because I was only 8, so were the other girls. They didn't know what they were saying or why. We were just kids.

There is so much evidence in both the psychological and spiritual realms that show how we unconsciously live through our childhood emotions again and again as we age. Our bodies are well developed, we run households and businesses, and we develop relationships, but a part of us is often still operating out of a 5-year-old's simple logic, the misinterpretations of a 10-year-old, or the misunderstandings of a 21-year-old. We've got to get in touch with those inner selves so that we're not contaminating new experiences with old thinking. In your growth process, you'll need to examine the relationships between who you are today and the invisible shackles that are tying you to the past.

CONJURED COURAGE

It's much easier to avoid reflecting on former situations. Some people don't want to relive the past. They're afraid of the humiliation and pain they once suffered, or they're afraid of facing the truth. It's important to know that going through that reflection process doesn't have any more power over you than what you give it. Those sometimes-painful memories are just stories about what happened, way back then. The fact that you're alive today means that those situations didn't destroy you. If you have the gumption to get out of bed everyday and provide for yourself, then the issues of your past don't have as much control over you as you might initially think.

Courage is an interesting thing. Perhaps we've been brainwashed into believing that courage comes only in big packages like an athlete making a comeback to win the championship or a mother of young children surviving a disease that was supposed to be fatal. Agreed, these acts take a great amount of courage, but so does finding gratitude when you only have fifty dollars in the bank and you're unsure if the electricity will still be on after Friday. It takes courage to get up in the morning when depression and heartache hover over you. If you're dealing with weight issues or you're uncomfortable with your appearance, it takes courage to put one foot before the other as you walk out to face the world.

Courage comes in big packages and in tiny, minuscule ones too. The size of courage doesn't matter; it's the fact that we use our strength to get up and seek it that matters. It will take courage for you to move forward with the processes in this book, as you might confront hard truths.

WHERE DID IT BEGIN?

I want you to imagine your mind as a flexible rubber band. Feel the elasticity and looseness. Try not to rigidly hold on to any ideas or thoughts, just let them come to you and manage them through the following exercises.

Before we stretch the mind and dive into this review, be mindful that you are in a learning process and it would be very kind of you to choose to hold a great amount of respect for yourself as you approach this. Carve out some time and lend your total attention to this exercise.

You will likely find some very interesting data which can lead you to a greater understanding of your feelings, reactions and choices.

I must preface that I really began to explore the emotional connections to the past after attending a forum with an international training and development company, Landmark Education. I soon encountered this past-present connection again in various books, psychology articles, and seminars. It showed up again through leadership training events led by entrepreneur and author George Zalucki. I also studied and absorbed information from international life coach Tony Robbins and his analogy of past belief systems and how we mismanage ourselves today based on old, often erroneous information of the past.

As I proceeded with my research into the subject of self-management and self-worth, I was so intrigued with the process and end result that I personally designed the below diagrams to help me see these cycles. I needed to post something on my wall to give me a clear look at myself and point out a recurring theme that was preventing me from achieving true power.

Exercise: **Step 1:** Take a look at each age box in Strut Figure 1: IDENTIFYING FOUR EMOTIONAL PATTERNS.

In the circle under each box, summarize one off-putting event that happened to you during this time. That event should be something that told you your world had changed forever, told you that everything wasn't OK, brought a big realization to you, or introduced you to great challenges or suffering. The event could be big or small, and could be something that has often come to mind for you in the years since it happened.

Write the event in the circle under each corresponding age box, and do this for each age category.

There may be some age boxes without a corresponding event, but I've found that most of us have at least a small incident that we can report for each of these ages. (Please note, this exercise can also be completed using positive events that changed your perspective of the world, but my goal here is to help you see how negative events help shape our emotions and build into the story we keep telling ourselves.)

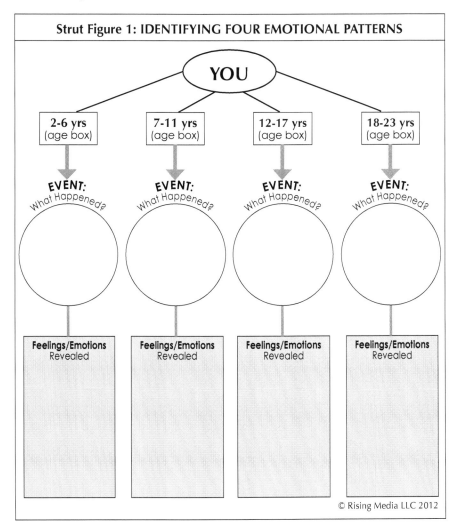

Strut Figure 1: IDENTIFYING FOUR EMOTIONAL PATTERNS

© Rising Media LLC 2012

Step 2: In Strut Figure 1, the rectangular box beneath each event circle list a few of the feelings that are associated with that incident for you. For example: see the following example based on the locker room story I shared previously.

Step 3: From Strut Figure 1, pick any one of the events from your diagram to work with for the next part of this exercise. You can, and I encourage you to, come back and work with each event but for now, review one at a time to keep from getting overwhelmed and discouraged from moving forward.

Step 4: In Strut Figure 2- write your chosen event in the event circle. Next, in the square box, write in the feelings/emotions associated with event (you listed these previously in Figure 1)

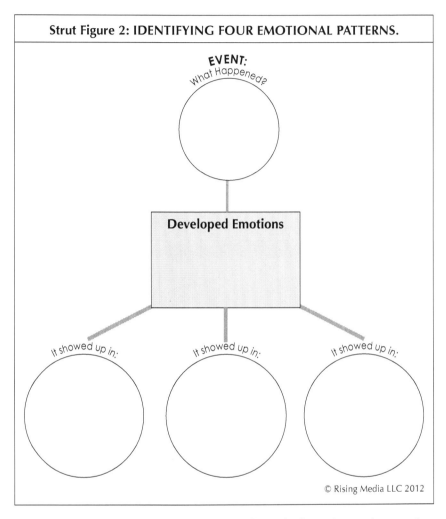

Strut Figure 2: IDENTIFYING FOUR EMOTIONAL PATTERNS.

EVENT:
What Happened?

Developed Emotions

It showed up in: It showed up in: It showed up in:

© Rising Media LLC 2012

Step 5: Working on the last row of circles titled "It Showed Up In"…
Think of how these feelings, assumptions, or interpretations that you
formed may have spilled over to other areas of your life such as work,
marriage or other areas. For instance, see the following example from
the locker room incident. Notice how the emotions I developed from
that event continued to play out in other areas of my life. It is a method
of connecting the dots. Look for a thread of connectivity that has
woven in and out of your life. You might need to go deeper than your
original thought. Often these old patterns show back up in a variety

of ways. Comb through your own story based on the information you've gathered here and see if you can connect certain feelings or behaviors to disempowering actions of past or present experiences.

Like me, you could very well be operating out of old feelings and patterns that you conjured up in your 5 or 12-year old mind. I can't express how important it is to really search deeply to find a running theme in your life as it connects to old patterns and old stories you've been telling yourself.

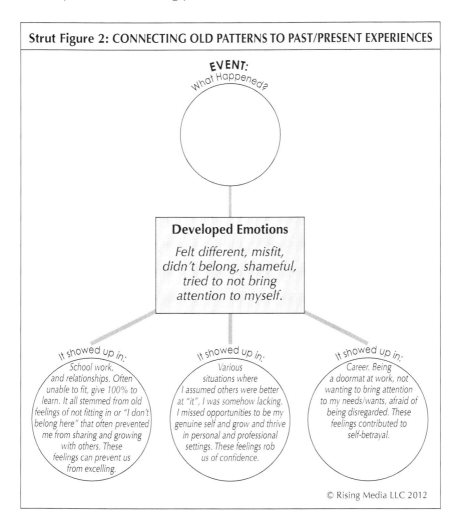

Strut Figure 2: CONNECTING OLD PATTERNS TO PAST/PRESENT EXPERIENCES

EVENT:
What Happened?

Developed Emotions

Felt different, misfit, didn't belong, shameful, tried to not bring attention to myself.

It showed up in:
School work, and relationships. Often unable to fit, give 100% to learn. It all stemmed from old feelings of not fitting in or "I don't belong here" that often prevented me from sharing and growing with others. These feelings can prevent us from excelling.

It showed up in:
Various situations where I assumed others were better at "it", I was somehow lacking. I missed opportunities to be my genuine self and grow and thrive in personal and professional settings. These feelings rob us of confidence.

It showed up in:
Career. Being a doormat at work, not wanting to bring attention to my needs/wants, afraid of being disregarded. These feelings contributed to self-betrayal.

© Rising Media LLC 2012

OUT OF FOCUS

Living your life with the emotional outlook of an 8-year-old is risky on many fronts. First, at the age of eight, we're still developing: medical doctors say that our brain isn't fully developed until we reach our mid-twenties. So whatever feelings we developed back in childhood were simply coping mechanisms to deal with the problem at hand. Our "age eight logic" is how we made sense of the dilemmas and pressure around us.

Some people were privy to a very sound and structured support system from a very young age. Some of you may have grown up in homes where the adults around you were introspective and transformative thinkers and you were brought up to be aware of the inner power that can override worldly suffering or maybe it was an auntie, teacher or grandparent. Most of us weren't raised by such people, though. We were raised by people who were also wounded, and who couldn't teach us better because they didn't know better. They didn't know how to stop their own pain. Their childhood interpretations spilled over into their twenties, thirties, and seventies. Some of them even lived their entire lives through the viewpoint of their eight-year-old selves.

Banking on our childhood point of view is blurry and that fuzziness usually rolls over into life and how we see things today. That means you're missing out on seeing beautiful things in others and in yourself. You might be passing up true love because after all, "how could someone love someone like me who isn't good enough for them?" (Or insert your own old pattern here.)

THE BIG LIE

Living life through these old patterns not only wastes a lot of precious time, it's damaging, and, at heart, it's all based on a lie.

Take my situation in the locker room. The fact is that the girl made the statement, that is true, but the lie stands in the feelings I developed because of it. I am not a misfit. One race isn't better than another. We're all equal. My feelings of worthlessness and not fitting in felt true to me for so many years because I'd been telling myself the same story over and over again. What we're really doing when we do this is perpetuating an old cycle. We're keeping our negative thoughts about ourselves alive and sometimes using those thoughts to make excuses for why things don't work out right or why life is so hard. It's time to get over these feelings and see them for what they really are--a big lie.

The big lie starts in childhood with the way that our emotionally immature mind makes everything mean something, and continues with our thoughts from that time of youth still buried within us, attaching themselves to our current situations and experiences. We can't undo what's been done, but we can cut the cord of chaotic connections of the past. We can see those childish thoughts of negativity as they really are and release them. You can choose to take your power back from what happened to you, just by gently agreeing that your experiences do not define you, they are just things that happened to you.

UNWRITING HISTORY

Trying to figure out why he beat you, why she ignored you, or why he ran away from home, leaving you to fend for yourself, isn't important. We can't answer for the perpetrator but we can stop playing victim.

I grew up in a family that most people would label as dysfunctional. I witnessed a lot of self-destruction and too much violence for even the toughest of kids to have to see. The people in my immediate circle didn't have a clue on how to undo what was done to them. Did these experiences play out in the adult years of those around me? Absolutely. What your mother, father, brother, or neighbor said or did to you was more than likely a learned pattern embedded inside of them, that turned into their way of coping with the stress of the situation at hand. There wasn't anything in you that made that person treat you like they did. When we are children, we're often unable to fend for ourselves, and we react in certain ways for a variety of reasons. Some of us fight back with violence, others bite their tongues and swallow their anger, and others turned to drugs or promiscuity.

Understanding that our families had their own built-up dramas before we got here is crucial. It's crucial because it allows us to dump a lot of harsh feelings that have been buckled on our backs, solidified in our minds, and branded in our hearts.

It wasn't until my late twenties that I really began to understand my great-grandmother and all of the pinned-up stories she lived through. Once I understood more about her, I was able to see her through a very different perspective.

She died in 1999 and kept a tight lip to the end on many secret dramas of this family I was born into. There are many things I will never know or get answers to, and I have to be OK with that. I can only be at peace with old family matters by knowing that most of my relatives were also living through old, harbored feelings and trying their best to live by what they believed was right. I had to learn to let go of any grievances and know who I am and recognize that I am not limited by any of the past conditions that happened to me.

KNOWING WHO YOU ARE NOT

After completing the Emotions and Patterns diagrams and gaining insight on the thoughts you created out of your four- or nine-year-old self, you now have a greater foundation on which to stand and explore. You can learn more about your genuine self by peeling away who you are not.

If you are not unworthy, stupid, mean, angry, hateful, or any of the lies we've been telling ourselves, then what traits do you possess? Who are you beyond the labels that people--even your own self--stamp into your conscience? Begin looking for evidence in your life to reveal who you are outside of those preconceived notions.

I'll never forget when I got introduced--excuse me, reintroduced, as she was always there--to my courageous self. I was attending a twelve-hour seminar, where the facilitator was talking about finding your authentic self. She related this concept to theories of some elite professors. She instructed the seminar participants to go deeper into our thoughts and mentally connect the dots that reappear in our lives. She repeated it, "go deeper," and on her fourth invocation of that key phrase, something popped within me. Before I knew it I was standing up at one of the microphones provided for attendee participation.

Through tears of joy, I shared a brief story about my past and how various experiences had left an ugly residue in me of things I couldn't shake. The facilitator began coaching me, guiding me through a process of old feelings versus new decisions. She reminded me of the courage that it took to get up in front of two hundred strangers and share a rather unappealing story, to take responsibility for my old thoughts and declare new victories. And she was right. Had I witnessed another person doing the same as I did, I certainly would've thought she was courageous for sharing such a personal side of herself.

So I pass the baton on to you. Think deeper, and then go even deeper than that. If you are not an arrogant woman, a misfit, a troublemaker, a gossiping queen, or unworthy, then what significance do you hold? Releasing past perceptions leaves plenty of room for something new, what do you now bring to yourself and to others in the present moment, who are you capable of being when you release the old voice of the past?

VOP vs. VIP

The voice of the past ("VOP") is confronted with the voice in the present ("VIP") as you excitedly work toward unraveling old marks on your psyche. Once you get your language right and begin projecting positively on yourself, it's like lathering the spirit in a super moist body cream that doesn't dissolve. You start to feel great about the skin you're in.

Talk yourself up at every opportunity you get. If you don't try anything else from this book, try this one thing: give yourself a verbal "praise party" every day, at least once a day. I recommend doing this every chance you get, before Morning Prayer or meditation, anytime you're looking in the mirror, while you're loading the dishwasher, or when driving in the car. Get into a groove of affirming, positive thoughts and make sure you're speaking your praises into the now by using present statements: "I am deserving of greatness", rather than, "I will be great at this".

No matter how often that voice in your head says "what's done is done," "you're too old for this, you can't change," "you can't do that because you don't have a college degree," or "no one will take you seriously," recognize that that's the VOP getting down on you, and you need to replace that VOP with a VIP power thought of affirmation and can-do determination.

In the introduction, I mentioned certain family members and how they would tell me I wouldn't have any good luck because of my unwillingness to go along with their agenda. I had to undo the thoughts of supposed bad luck by saying and believing, "I am worthy of goodness," and "great things flow to me easily and effortlessly," over and over again. I had to do more than just believe these affirmations; I had to really feel them in my soul. In the following Strutting Stones, you'll find three ways to increase your VIP and shut down your VOP.

This program works only if you make it work. Some days are easier than others, but when you bring intention to the way you are living your life, whether through VOP or VIP, it's going to take patience and time to get to where you want to be. You might master the erasing of the VOP for days, weeks, or even months and then one day, it pops back up again. So what? That VOP appearance doesn't mean anything, it's just another opportunity to practice tightening your mindfulness muscle.

DAILY ACCESS

Surround yourself with people and things that represent, respond to, and reinforce the traits that you are discovering within yourself. From the friends on your speed-dial to the paintings on your wall, everything around you should lift your life and support your new outlook. Your surroundings need to be in sync with your intention to flourish.

I was coaching a client who wanted to work on feelings and a negative belief system she had about herself. One of things she wanted to remove from her psyche was the thought that she was lazy. She was having a hard time finding a job and her eight-year-old self was telling her that she was lazy. While that wasn't true--she actually had accomplished a lot in life--her energy was low at that time.

I took inventory of her living space and, wouldn't you know it, in her very organized living room, right next to the telephone, was a pen and pad. The colorful notepad had a picture of a woman lying in the grass with a breezy sundress fanned out on the ground around her. The inscription on each page? "I wasn't meant to work." Cute! But not reinforcing the right outlook for this woman who was already battling lackadaisical feelings. Something as small as a slogan on a notepad that sidetracks your purpose can cause problems in your efforts to plow forward and improve yourself.

Carve out a little time and make a list of things that are prominent in your life and meaningful to who you are now. Double-check that list against the person you are striving to be and ask yourself if each item is in alignment with the direction you're heading. If it isn't, it's time to discard it, give it away, sell it, or whatever you need to do to let it go because it's not serving you. When something isn't serving you, it's disserving you.

There was a time during my television news career when I was relocating every couple of years, so I stored many of my household items. When I left that part of my career behind, I also left ninety percent of those things in storage--I'd gotten along without them for so long, I would just go back and pull them out later. Four years later, my husband and I cleaned out our storage space and I began unwrapping various pieces of framed art and miniature statues, most of which did not resonate with me anymore. I collected and accumulated these things during a time in my life when I was living in uncertainty, and some of the pieces that spoke to me then reflected that lack of direction. I can see that connection between my mindset and my purchases today, but couldn't back then. It's now obvious that I was drawn to some of those items years ago because they spoke to how I felt about my life and the world.

Today, I am a different woman; my life has changed because I have changed. Some wounds have turned to blessings and bitterness to love, so there just isn't room in my life for objects that don't support that. I slowly purchased new things that resembled me and the world I believed in and things that strengthened me.

We all need a space of cohesiveness, so consider making your home a sanctuary that fulfills and supports your mental needs. Self-awareness is about more than just tending to self, we should honor our living space as well.

The rest of principles listed in this book are the tools needed for uncovering the things we no longer need to hold on to and the tools needed to help you identify exactly what you do need and how to get it.

❊ STRUTTING STONES ❊

1. Without stopping to ponder, quickly think of three instances in life where you felt strong, smart, and victorious. Write them in the space below.

   1.

   2.

   3.

2. From the information you provided above, can you identify

with what was happening in your life during those times? Think about your energy level. Who was around? What did you see, hear, and smell? Recreate this time as much as you can and use that information to help you identify with characteristics you have, but may not have daily access to.

3. Spiritual leader and author, Louise Hay reminds us, in "You Can Heal Your Life", that we replay worry and stress over and over in our minds. Replacing that negative affirmation with a positive one isn't too much to ask and is a much better use of our brain space. What disempowering affirmation do you need to release and what are you willing to replace it with?

4. What was the most surprising element in the Emotion/Patterns work in Figure 1 and 2? What was the most fascinating thing you learned about yourself by reviewing past events?

5. Did you notice any old belief systems that you may have used to hide behind or make excuses for yourself? If so, list each one of them and own up to it and understand that those actions are a thing of the past, they have no hold on you whatsoever, only what you choose to give to it.

6. Here are three ways to strengthen your VIP. I post these in my office or copy them on a note and carry in my purse just as an instructional reminder on how to keep the energy flowing toward my VIP.

1. Recognize who's talking: VOP or VIP

2. Acknowledge any negativity and gently let it go (avoid being hard on yourself).

3. Replace the negative thoughts with new positive VIP statements, (I am deserving of greatness", etc.)

3

PREFERENTIAL PARDON

"Resentment is like taking poison and hoping the other person dies." ~ *St. Augustine*

Strutting your stuff is a collaboration of purposeful living and surge in power. It's a generous regard of your highest self, which can get congested when you're harboring emotional upset with yourself or others. When we're in a state of unforgiveness we are, in fact, in a state of spiritual suicide. We're cutting off our supply of joy and robbing ourselves of the opportunity to progress.

Through life's ups and downs, we can easily become our own punching bag. "I can't believe I did that!" "What a stupid thing to say, what was I thinking?" This disempowering language prevents us from becoming--and staying--friendly with ourselves. Becoming your own friend is something you can master, no matter how much torment you've survived. You can establish a beautiful, loving connection with yourself, even if you're still striving to become the person that you know you are meant to be.

I don't know about you, but I've done some pretty foolish things in the past. I walked away from a high-paying job, with no set back-up plan. I made a decision to team up with a couple in a marketing business venture, and those people ended up conning me out of a little bit of cash and betraying what I thought was genuine friendship. I burped while having lunch with the top news anchorman in my area. The list keeps going--I could probably give you enough of my gaffes to compete with the number of pages in this book.

But as we know, to err is human. Somewhere in our minds, we don't really believe that...we don't accept it...if we did, we would be better at forgiving ourselves as well as others. We must forgive all the way or forget it.

There is no numeral percentage to forgiveness, you can't forgive someone a little bit or eighty-five percent- it's all the way or nothing at all. When you decide to totally let it go and move beyond the abrasiveness of resentment, you'll be faced to make a decision, one that defines your personal boundaries surrounding the person or people involved in the act.

If you have allowed someone to hurt you, or you have hurt yourself, you have the right to understand why you hurt, how you hurt, and how hurt like that can be prevented in the future.

Looking into the reason why you hurt is another self-examination of feelings, thoughts, and past behavior. Seeking the "how" in a painful episode helps you to observe and analyze situations and chart how things can escalate to trouble. Prevention can only come after you have examined the how's and the why's.

WHAT'S THE POINT?

People can sure make you mad. They can stir up your temper faster than you can say, "fried green tomatoes". Before you know it, the words and actions of others cut right through you, and the last thing you're interested in is forgiving them.

It's not about them or--if I can get a little "down home" here--it ain't about them, it's about you. Let's agree on something, you are not a fool. You will not continue to allow someone to keep causing pain and grief at your expense, right? You must guard yourself from such people, but foolishness has a way of sneaking back up on you. Before long, once again you're right back in the predicament you promised you'd never revisit. Your temper has flared and all of your emotions are right back up at the boiling point.

It does you absolutely no good to stir in animosity. Anger deflates your power, not that of the person you're angry with. The energy you spend on the situation usually doesn't affect the man or woman you're angry with. They might not even know that you are angry at them!

Wasting your energy in fruitless rage is one thing, but another sad outcome of anger is that you can create a blockage in your mind. Goodness may be trying to knock on your heart, but that heart is closed by the corrosion of anger. Great things can't enter a mind preoccupied with rage and revenge. Staying fixated on unforgiveness creates a hate-filled world, keeping life's positive gifts away.

I once encountered a woman during one of my seminars who later confessed to me privately that her father had raped her when she was a child. She was now near seventy years old and was still holding on to the tormented feelings from this tragic, cruel attack. Her father had been dead for nearly forty years but the woman was conjuring up the fresh pain of an old wound. She was aware that he was dead but couldn't understand why he still had such a hold on her. She admitted to not wanting to forgive him because what he did was so terribly wrong.

I agreed that what he did to her was unfathomable and she didn't deserve it, but continuing to hold on to it makes her a servant to his brutality, not a victor over it. The energy this woman used in hating her father could've been instead used for uplifting that little girl who was still very much scorned and in need of attention and affirmation. I encouraged the woman to at least put herself in a place of considering forgiveness toward her father, not because he needed it, but because she did. *It was time for her to love herself more than she hated him.*

I went through a few exercises with this woman during our time together, to demonstrate where in her life she had forfeited opportunities due to the strong hold her father maintained over her. She began to see that she was only hurting herself, regardless of whether her father was dead or alive. She couldn't hurt him with her deep-seated grudge, even though her anger was righteous. All of this anguish was bottled up inside of her, and for years she had allowed it to dictate a life that focused on the negative. It was as if her father was committing the act on her over and over again, for forty or fifty years. She kept reliving it and bringing herself to an agonizing level of pain, sorrow, and pity.

We figure these things out when we're twenty, forty, eighty years old, or sometimes not at all--some people die with long-endured malice in their hearts. There is no need for you to be carrying these negative affirmations any longer, what's the point? Release them. Do it for yourself, do it for that little girl inside of you or the curious teen you once were, and do it for the woman that you are today. You deserve to be free of animosity, and you are so very deserving of goodness.

LESSONS IN FORGIVENESS

There are many layers to resentment and why we feel the way we do. There are also layers of lessons within those long-harbored feelings. We often don't get to learn these lessons because it hurts too much to dig that deep into old slights and hurts. We might scratch the surface and feel that unpleasant memory rise again. Because we don't want to relive that bad time, we suppress it again. We're not healing ourselves by covering up our fury again; the only way to get to a more peaceful, resolved place is by going through the pain of past situations. There is no other way to resolve our anger.

So let's start with the good news. Within the thick walls of unforgiveness are stored lessons. These lessons are very valuable and there are many of them, but they are temporarily hidden from us in the shadow of resentment. Now is the time to crack the surface of that anger and slowly start chipping away toward the valuable lessons within. You may unearth some amazing things about yourself and about the people in your life. Once you discover these truths, you'll label that former hatred as it really was--not missed opportunity or failure, but as a lesson learned.

Women who are serious about the pursuit of their strut are determined to reach that desired destination. We use all of the information at our disposal to better ourselves, not belittle ourselves.

Consider making a definitive decision to finally let go of the things you've been holding against yourself and others. There is more on this is in the following Strutting Stones section.

The absolute best thing about learning from experiences is it teaches us how to better connect with others. It strengthens our sensitivities and ability to empathize with one another. For everything you've gone through, I can guarantee that a large percentage of those experiences--good and bad--have shaped your ability to connect with others.

Learn the lesson behind a grudge or resentment you've been holding and then let that anger go and let yourself grow. Use the lesson for yourself; use it to understand, or even help, others during their own difficult times.

FORGIVE BUT KEEP IT REAL

By the standard definition, forgiveness means to cease to feel resentment against an offender, to give pardon, it does not mean to pretend like the act never happened. In the book "A Course In Miracles" there are practical lessons and applications for forgiveness as it relates to spiritual enlightenment. The book suggests that forgiveness is a form of a miracle that transforms our minds from disempowering thoughts and restores our minds to peace and joy.

In the Course, it is suggested that we live in the truth of forgiveness over the attack of suffering through it, we must let go of all of the blame, guilt and anger and embrace a more holistic approach and a more loving approach. In seeking total resolve in forgiveness we are setting ourselves and the perpetrator free but it doesn't mean that we must overlook the act and pretend that it never happened. We don't hold a grudge nor do we hold the door open for the act to happen again.

I've received many letters and emails from both men and women who are working on forgiving family members who violated them in their early years. Most of those notes question the difficulty of being around the perpetrator and trying to please other relatives who pretend these acts never happened.

"How can I show up at the family reunion with my kids and sit next to my uncle, laughing and smiling and pretending like he didn't rape me," one woman wrote. "How can I go along with everyone else while inside, I'm a shaking, scared, mad ten-year old with anxiety about what this man did to me?" one man asked. Another person asked about forgiving a boss who talks down on others or a friend who betrays their trust.

My short answer: You don't have to pretend anything and you don't have to break bread with him. Forgiving a person in no way means the harm they brought on you is OK. Dismissing the act doesn't mean that you must allow them back into your life.

It is your choice on how you handle the actions post-forgiveness. If it's healthier for you to avoid the perpetrator, do that and don't allow naysayers to talk you out of it. You know you're breaking point, honor what your instinct is telling you. If you choose to avoid a relationship with the person, that doesn't mean that you're still mad or that you haven't truly forgiven him, it simply means that you have to honor your higher self and chumming it up with that person may not feel authentic to you.

No matter what someone did or didn't do, we can release our attachment to what happened and release the thoughts associated with it and we may also choose to let it go and let that person go as well.

SPECIAL DELIVERY

Yes, the old advice still works: writing a letter to yourself or the person you're in need of forgiving, whether or not you ultimately choose to share your words with that person. Your letter can start with a simple "Dear ___, I'm willing to forgive you for _____." You can continue your letter from there in any way that helps you--you can say things that you've been wanting to say, or refuse to say much more than that you're taking your power back. Letter-writing is a powerful form of release. It helps us to articulate our feelings, fine-tune our message, and communicate exactly what we want the other person to hear.

This is a mock letter of a woman who was emotionally and physically abused by her stepfather, who also hurt her two younger sisters and their mother.

> *Dear "Joe":*
>
> *I have made the decision to forgive you for abusing me, my sisters, and my mother. I realize that I didn't deserve any of it. None of us did. You were the one with the problem, and I can't help you. Your problem is not my fault.*
>
> *You can not hurt me again, nor will I allow memories of you to hurt me. What you did to me was wrong and you'll have to face those consequences one day but I have found out how very strong I was then and still am. You didn't win over me. I survived the worst you could offer, and I have become a stronger person through that hellish experience at the hands of someone who was supposed to love me.*
>
> *You called me names that hurt back then, but I am not what you said. I never was. I now understand that all of your ranting and raving, all your name-calling and putdowns,*

reflected was how you felt about yourself. No real man speaks so cruelly to the vulnerable members of his family. You were the coward, not me. You had the problem with life beating you up, not me.

I will never be able to go back and undo all of the pain you caused, but I can forgive you. I forgive you because, even after all of the damage you caused, I still have a heart. In my heart I know that I am choosing to release the power you once had over us, through forgiveness.

I don't want to ever see you again and you certainly are not welcome in my home. I don't wish anyone the treatment you gave to me and my family, and I really don't wish you harm. However, today is the day that I release you and release my resentment over what you did to us. I release it so that I may have a loving relationship with my husband, I release it so that I may be fully present with my two wonderful children, and I release it for myself and the strength that I use to survive.
Strongly Written,
"Karen"

I first learned the power of letter-writing when I began seeing a grief counselor after two close relatives unexpectedly died a few months apart. There were things I didn't get a chance to say to them, so the therapist introduced me to the power of letter-writing. She also suggested that it could be used for other healing reasons, such as the forgiveness for which I'm recommending it here.

The key is the no-holds-barred approach. Say what you mean to say and take back whatever power you may have relinquished (knowingly or unknowingly) to that person. Don't sugarcoat the situation, call it as you see it.

Next, get into the body of the letter and bring up your feelings. What did that person's actions do to you? What did that person take from you? What questions do you have surrounding the incident or the person? Bring up whatever you need to in this section.

Finally, end the letter with a declaration statement. Reclaim yourself by taking back your power from the event/person and note that you are not a victim, but a victor.

Re-read the letter to yourself and let whatever emotions and thoughts arise wash over you. Re-read your words a third time, a tenth time, or as many times as you need to. Read this heartfelt letter until you feel something move aside and release inside of you, leaving a lighter sensation than before.

I don't suggest that you mail or email the letter unless you are prepared for a hostile reaction or no reaction at all. This process is really all about you coughing up these feelings, bringing them to the surface and dealing with them in your own private way. I've often burned these letters after they helped me finally let anger go. I buried one many years ago near my childhood home, unsigned and undelivered, but there was meaning for me behind that burial ceremony.

You should deliver the information to yourself the best way you can--with kindness and thoughtfulness. This is a delicate process so give yourself plenty of time, in a relaxing, quiet, private place, maybe over several days to work through your writing and reflection process.

GENTLENESS

When you're caring for a newborn baby, you're careful how you touch him, you don't squeeze her too tightly, and you don't yank him suddenly from the crib. During feedings, you give him just enough, careful not to overdo it. And when you look at this new baby, you have some emotions. Maybe you are joyful, or hopeful, or both. Maybe you're overwhelmed by the miracle before your eyes; you may even think about God's grace in sending you this little messenger.

Be this way with yourself as you take steps toward forgiveness. Choose to see yourself and the world differently. Pick your head up out of old circumstances, and be willing to let go of old grievances. Forget about the missed opportunities you weren't prepared for; avoid replaying that embarrassing situation at work or the time you made a scene in public. Gently let this forgiveness occur as carefully as you would cuddle a baby.

In your gentleness, when an unforgiving thought arises, simply acknowledge it and choose to release it. Counter it with the sage advice of civil rights activist and poet Dr. Maya Angelou: "when you know better, you do better". Choose to follow a new train of thought, because now you do know better.

We don't know everything and we surely don't get things right all of the time. Life is about learning. It's true that we do better--with ourselves and with others--when we know better, and that's all there is to it. We have to free this negativity or else we haven't truly forgiven ourselves. We don't lead powerfully when we're hurting. We don't make good decisions under anguish, either, so we must discontinue our need to marinate ourselves in such negative emotions. The mind, body, and soul are in upset when we wander in anger and let it control us.

When wounds of the past threaten to reopen, applying a little gentleness will go a long way. Anytime we can soften those memories of tough days with maturity, thought, and gentleness, we're a step ahead of the game. There is an old song that encourages us to "try a little tenderness" and I think tenderness is exactly what we need to give ourselves.

BECOME YOUR OWN BBF

People who don't like themselves usually have a difficult time finding other people to like them. Folks who insist on seeing a messed-up, hateful world will usually find themselves mired in a pool of tragedies, mishaps, and hatefulness. What we think upon, we draw upon, and ultimately we become.

I've had many cool fall nights on my patio with a cup of tea and just me. I can treat myself to dinner without a companion and be totally OK with the company I'm in. Whether you don't like spending time with yourself, or if you find your own company to be pleasant and fun, other people will sense that and treat you accordingly.

Some people can't stand being alone. They obsessively check their cell phone even if it's not ringing. They'll insist on getting together with others solely to avoid time alone. They run to any- and everything to avoid themselves, only to still come up empty.

Other people cannot fill us up, and neither can things. A new purse won't give us fulfillment, and neither will a trip to Vegas. These little luxuries in life are beautiful and wonderful to experience but they don't draw a love line to your inner connectedness. We can learn to enjoy such activities and vacations by being in touch with ourselves, even if we are sharing the experiences with others. We can upgrade the thrill and super-size the outcome of any event, big or small, just by being friendly with ourselves. You will naturally enjoy life more when you find authentic joy within yourself.

Here's a simple strategy for embracing the friend within: think about friendship and what characteristics you seek in a friend, and become that to yourself.

What traits do you look for in a friend? What are some common characteristics that your good friends share? Now, take those traits on, yourself. If you seek honesty and fun, work on your truthfulness and ability to have fun--start with being honest with yourself and seeking out fun situations.

There really isn't any other way to befriend yourself. If you want something that's more promising and more productive, you've got to get more personal.

A young lady I once mentored was so dependent on others that she had no idea how to be with herself or accept time in her own company. I gave her the assignment of treating herself to lunch at her favorite restaurant and the rules were clear. She was to take one full hour, with no cell phone, no books, and no company. I advised her to just enjoy the meal and the company she kept.

It took this young woman three tries before she could actually do it. She told me, "people were looking at me like I was crazy, and I didn't want them to think that I don't have anyone to have lunch with." So she pulled out her cell phone and started texting.

After hearing about this first attempt, I asked my protégé, why she cared what the other restaurant patrons thought about her. I said to her, "and are they depositing love into your life, and are they responsible for taking care of you? They have nothing to do with you. You're making their looks or stares mean something because you're avoiding yourself." I asked this young lady, "how do you know they aren't admiring your courage for being alone? A lot of people wish they could be comfortable in that situation but they can't."

The next week she tried it again and, once again, gave into

embarrassment and assumptions about what other people "must" be thinking of her. She went to the car, got a book, and sat down at the lunch table pretending to study.

I really wanted this young lady to develop a friendship with herself because others were mistreating her. She couldn't really see it because she was mistreating herself as well. My goal in giving her this assignment was to pull her attention away from her routine and make her a little uncomfortable, so that she could begin to see where and why she was running from her self.

On the third week, she did it! She sat through an entire lunch alone without any disruptions. Her observations on this successful exercise were:

- I usually eat fast, but because I had an entire hour to fill, I slowed down and the food tasted different. I could taste seasonings that I didn't know were there.

- Most of the people in the restaurant looked really tired. No one looked happy.

- I had a nice waiter, a good-looking college kid. I talked to him a little and found out that he's working his way through business school. He gave me great eye contact and really good service.

- I have courage. I didn't know this until the lunch. While I was eating, I was able to think about some times in my life that I thought I was weak, but the very fact I was able to sit alone and be OK with a solo lunch tells me that I'm stronger than I realized.

- I need a manicure.

This woman clearly made the most out of that hour. She took some self-notes but she also had a chance to look at others and see her world from a different perspective. When we feel good about ourselves, when we have genuine love for ourselves, everything looks different. We have different conversations, even with strangers or a kind waiter--we even have a different dialogue with ourselves.

❋ STRUTTING STONES ❋

1. Finding Lessons in the Acts.

Recall two areas where you are carrying unresolved memories. Allow one of these episodes to be unforgiveness of self, and the other to be resentment you're holding toward another person. For example:

1. "I walked away from a good marriage for thoughtless reasons."

2. "My grandfather was abusive to me."

Looking squarely at these two examples, our first reactions could easily be pain and overwhelming sorrow, but if we look closer, we'll also be able to learn things about ourselves that will helps us grow. We can break through the resentment like an eggshell and reveal incredible lessons that can't be bought, but can only be earned. Harvesting lessons through this process sticks with us because we had to experience so much pain to get the benefit. We have the capability to learn a lot through painful episodes because we don't want to feel that sort of pain again. Therefore, we can capitalize on the pain triggers to teach us how to avoid them in the future.

Back to the example, let's flip this agonizing list to focus on the lessons learned:

1. If you left the relationship then later regretted your decision, it's time to look at the lesson you learned so that you won't repeat it or keep replaying it. Perhaps a person who encountered this painful event can learn about relationships and how to communicate with others, in both romantic and friendship contexts. Maybe a person in this type of situation can also give some thought to boundary-setting and mindful thinking strategies to help her understand rash decisions versus planned and executed tasks and events.

2. Abusive relatives is a hard history to overcome. It doesn't matter if the abuse was physical, emotional, sexual, or some combination, it's hard on any child to grow up and forgive all that the abuser(s) have taken away. For the (former) child who can do this, though, there are powerful lessons lingering in the forgiveness process.
You can certainly learn how to, and how not to, treat others. There are also lessons about love and how to express it appropriately, even when life is rough or times are hard. You can also understand how important it is to speak up for yourself and always value yourself no matter what.

2. With a new perspective of past events, write down the lessons learned from the act or you may find a valuable lesson in the actual act of forgiving yourself or another person.

3. Think about a situation where you think you need forgiveness
in your life, either of yourself or others, List three benefits you are
getting from holding on to them.

1.

2.

3.

4. List three benefits of releasing it.

1.

2.

3.

5. Write a letter to someone who has wronged you. Follow the
outline of the example letter provided previously in this chapter.
After writing it out and reading it as many times as you need to,
what emotions did you feel? Did you feel a shift in your thinking
or heart?

6. In becoming your own friend, what three qualities do you admire
about yourself?

1.

2.

3.

And list one trait you would like to work on.

    1.

7. Who do you need to forgive and what steps are you willing to put into action to calm the pains of the past?

4

PACIFYING POISON PEOPLE

Some people will drum up several reasons why they don't like you, and none of those reasons have any bearings on you, your ability to excel, or the purpose you are here to serve.

You can't make people see something that they don't want to see. My back-story of growing up in a fatherless house, raised by three women--Mom, Grandmother, and Great-Grandmother--was something most of us kids in that neighborhood had in common. Playing kickball and hide-n-seek until the wee hours of those hot, sticky summery nights are things we all did. We collected pop bottles to capture the fascination of lightning bugs, we chalked up our sidewalks with championship hopscotch drawings, and we played imaginary millionaires with Monopoly money. And when we got into trouble, we all were corrected. My mother could punish the kids down the street if needed, just like their parents could me. If my great-grandmother hit one cousin with a willow switch, I got it too. I was no exception to the scolding

If I had a dollar for every time I heard from someone in my life say, "you think you're better than everyone else," or "you don't understand because you've always had it easy," I'd be able to feed a small country for a week. My initial response used to be this screeching high-pitched scream that's reminiscent of a woman in distress. Although this scream was completely internal (and, I'd like to think, normal), it was my first reaction to a very frustrating presumption from my accuser.

On the outside, I'd purse my lips together and force a mechanical smile with a quick rebuttal to their accusation: "we all grew up together, with the same challenges, in the same neighborhood, there's no one better than the other." But they often quickly had a response and needed to get in the last word: "yeah, but you were different".

I couldn't see their take on my differences. I couldn't fathom a line drawn with me on one side and a team of "them" on the other side. Their accusations of me used to infuriate me. I used to get angry at the very thought of how much pain I endured from my early years on as I worked toward a career, and life, that was my goal. I would get mad that these teasing relatives, friends, classmates or neighbors who didn't--or couldn't--see me for who I really was. I tried to convince emotionally blinded, stuck-in-the past associates that my hardships were just as real as theirs. I took on more and more guilt and discomfort until I realized that there was nothing I could do to change their minds--they were convinced that they knew my story better than I did. No matter how many encouraging columns I wrote, self-empowerment speeches I gave, or interviews I gave about my struggle to know myself, their minds were made up.

In my weekly newspaper column, I mainly focus on inspirational and empowerment topics, but I've also written about my climbs and falls. I've shared personal stories of conflict and resolution in my own life, but some of those people obviously weren't reading about those struggles. I have traveled the country speaking at various seminars and workshops about how I decided to steer my own course in life and worked to get there, and yet those people from my past weren't present at those events. I've developed and facilitated corporate training events to help others benefit from the lessons I've learned, and--yet again--those naysayers didn't show up for that, or else they would've heard my story and my truth. But then again, would that have made any difference? Would it have changed their minds at all? Now that I reflect on the negative personalities pointing the finger of entitlement at me, my guess is, probably not.

I knew my story and how it affected me. Regardless if others accepted it or not wasn't my problem. I learned in my late twenties that trying to convince others of something makes me just as much a part of their foolishness as they are. I can't pacify a person stuck in poisonous thoughts and negative impressions; their way is their way.

Rendering yourself powerless in order to please someone else will leave you spiritually bankrupt, emotionally hijacked, and physically depleted. When we lock away the specialness inside of us, we're destroying a gift or talent or idea that was planted in us long before now, and to deny that truth for the benefit of a jealous or angry person is ludicrous.

If you choose to pacify that poisonous person, you're setting up a powerful trap, even if you don't realize it. What you are essentially saying is that his needs are more important than your own needs; her desire to put you down or ridicule you is more important than your own desire to grow and advance. Which you and I both know is not the truth.

I don't use the word "poison" loosely. People who spit on your ideas and attempt to kill your dreams are spreading a poisonous energy that can kill your ambition. This poison of negativity can put a sneaky chokehold on your dreams before you even see it coming.

IDENTIFYING THE MOB

Unlocking the significance of your strut often means treading your path solo. There isn't a buddy system here, because no one can completely identify with your issues the way you can. And if you look to your inner circle for support, you probably won't find much unless you have already aligned yourself with people who are striving to grow--those who are accountability partners or mentors.

The hard-to-digest truth is that some people are wading in a cesspool of negativity. They're waiting to see you fail. They might work with you, eat dinner with you or even be sleeping next to you. Girls' night out might also carry some venomous friends. The man or woman who sits next to you in the pew at church can be swollen with toxicity.

The pop culture calls these poisonous people "haters" based on their tendency to be jealous of others' looks or success, and their hatred in seeing others do well. Classify them as you wish, they still bear one thing in common: they are toxic poison to anyone with a plan of action, with a plan to achieve something more than what these people currently have. They are crippled in their mindset. Instead of doing the work to understand their hateful feelings, they prey on those who have something good in their lives and on those who are trying to improve their situations. My father calls them the Mob: a pack (small or large group) of people whose one aim is to bring you down, and once they succeed they move on to target the next achiever. The Mob is anyone that tries to move you away from being yourself, anyone who tries to pull you down. I've met members of the Mob throughout school, in professional settings and even at seminars and workshops. The Mob will always exist in some form or fashion but there are two important facts to remember. One, identify them so that you are aware of what you're dealing with and two, refuse to hand over your goods in order to soften their fights with failure. We can never allow the Mob to change our minds about the direction we're headed in or the life that we desire.

You can't change the Mob. I believe that, deep down, we know this, but something in us wants to give it a try. We think, "maybe if I include him more, he'll realize the importance of supporting my goals," or, "maybe if she could see how other people respect me at work, then she'll see me for who I am now and not who I used to be."

No matter what you do or what you don't do, it will never be enough to lift another person's head up out of the mud puddle, you are a go-getter you will want to be, and need to be, in the company of those of like minds. Trying to hang on to the Mob's small-mindedness handicaps your ability to see straight. Under their influence, you'll worry about your ability to think straight, and before you know it everything is confusing, you feel frustrated, and you have no idea why. You will have been poisoned by the energy radiating from toxic folks, who are experts at sucking the very life out of you. They can talk you out of your dreams quicker than a two-year-old can throw a tantrum.

Poisonous people come in all shapes, sizes, colors, economic backgrounds; they are from good neighborhoods, bad neighborhoods, great families, or no family at all. You might manage them or even be married to them. They might be your cousin or your mother. Toxicity can come from your father or your boss. Their venom might not necessarily be spewed at you--they can denounce others or berate themselves, but either way their negativity hobbles your progress, as you're trying to move forward and appease them at the same time. It'll never happen. It'll never, ever, happen.

I once knew a woman who wasn't putting me down, but she was overly abusive to herself. She talked badly about herself a lot, and I associated it with the unattended-to pain she had shared with me a few years earlier. When she would put herself down during our conversations, I tried to help her see that she could get past that negative self-talk, but she wasn't open to that. After a while, I simply got tired of hearing her berate herself or talk about how colleagues walked all over her. When I asked her, as a friend, "what are you going to do about the way they're treating you?" she lacked a response and didn't even seem interested in finding one. This woman wasn't motivated to grow or get past the situation, she just needed a sounding board and I was that for her. Well, a sounding board is just a blank block of wood, and this role wasn't good for me or the friendship. One day I simply said, "I can't do this any more. If you need to talk about yourself or colleagues in an insulting way, call someone else because I'm not longer available to participate in this form of abuse."

I didn't say, "I'm sorry" because I hadn't done anything wrong except honor myself and really honor her in a truthful way. We hung up, and, to this day, I haven't received another call from her.

I'm not angry with this woman, I wish her love and I hope that she was able to get past that cycle of negativity. It's like that line in the movie "Eat, Pray, Love" when Richard is speaking to Liz about her ex-husband, and he tells her it's OK to miss him and each time she does, to just send him love. I think that's the best thing we can do with people who are no longer a part of our lives: wish them love and peace. Sending these well wishes softens whatever displeasures may have happened in the past and paves the way for us to keep building on goodness and improving ourselves.

You are probably keenly aware of who is toxic in your life, but sometimes we might be so busy in trying to avoid them that we miss those who genuinely care for us and speak out of a place of concern or constructive criticism. The easiest way to decipher where seemingly negative comments are truly coming from is to listen closely for a few traits in the relationship. (Most members of the Mob will usually exhibit these attitudes/behaviors:

- Put- downs (of you or themselves)

- Often reminding you of your past errors or success and comparing it to a recent hardship.

- Making negative comments about your age, looks, resources, or anything that they feel will lower your chances of pursuing your goals.

- Mainly criticizing others, rarely brings good news.

GRANTING PERMISSION

When we want to advance, we are essentially promoting ourselves to new levels of spirituality and education. We're opening ourselves up to establishing greater potential, and we begin making executive decisions for our overall well-being. With all of the things we accept, we have to reject a few things as well. One of the first things you need to do is give yourself permission to leave poisonous people right where they are.

Avoid spending time and energy on judging someone else as wrong and yourself as right. It's not about what's "correct", it's about what's best for you. Stop spinning your wheels trying to prove a point. As the old saying goes, "Never argue with a fool, onlookers may not be able to tell the difference." If your situation is more complicated and you can't pry yourself away from that poisonous influence, then find someone else to share your ideas and goals with as you work to break free of the ridicule and darkness imposed by the toxic person. Sometimes you won't even need to work to leave the poisonous person behind. Don't be alarmed if this person is gently moved out of your life without your saying a word or doing anything. I so love it when the Universe works this way!

I had a childhood friend who I just adored and we continued a friendship well into our twenties, but then we just grew apart and she started to become toxic to me. I knew deep inside that her life was very different from mine and we just didn't have a lot in common anymore, but I desperately wanted to keep the friendship alive for old times' sake. It was hurtful to realize it was time to move on, but something told me to let her go without turning back. I soon began to find myself surrounded by new friends who shared similar interest and goals with me. Become comfortable with the notion that it's OK to move on, even if the people you are leaving behind may want the situation to remain unresolved.

WHY WE STAY

I have this memory of sitting cross-legged on the floor of my childhood home, eating popcorn while watching "The Jefferson's" on our big floor model TV while my great-grandfather sat in his cream-colored leather rocking chair with a horse's head design embroidered on the front seat cushion. A snowstorm brewed outside, but inside, the house was warm and quiet. Everything was OK and I felt protected and very safe. I was four or five years old.

That memory is so nostalgic because we have very strong connections to what's safe and comfortable. We know the situation and the outcome, so it's safe, with no risks involved. But as an adult, it's a different story. There are many times I have been out in the world taking on big decisions and choices, and I've felt exposed and afraid. Sometimes I've actually wished that I could go back to that old dusty living room and rest in the protection of my great-grandfather. But that is impossible.

If you're used to living or working around negative influences, you might feel a bit threatened at the idea of stepping out of that environment. It may seem very uncomfortable to leave the familiarity of that situation. Even if it causes you grief, you still might dread leaving. I believe that so many people, especially women, try to hang in there because we feel badly about moving on, or we regret that we can't share our dreams with the people we love.

In the 1957 Italian Romanic film "Nights of Cabiria" an older prostitute, Cabiria, played by Giulietta Masina, walks the streets of Rome looking for true love. She and some of her friends find their way to a church confessional and Cabiria admits to her friends that she wants to change, that she wants a better life. She kneels before a picture of The Madonna, lights candles, and cries out for help.

The movie moves to the next scene, where Cabiria and her friends are picnicking with music, food, and liquor Cabiria realizes that she and her group have returned right back to the same lifestyle as before.

"We haven't changed!" Cabiria screams out at the confused looking group, "we're all the same as before." She cries as she realizes the futility of her wish.

In the movie, her friends never agreed with her invitation to change, nor did they join her plea during the confessional. This was something that Cabiria alone wanted. Like most of us, she wanted to be part of a team, she wanted everyone to jump on the change train. It's so much more comfortable to have familiar folks around you while you're in unfamiliar territory. It's easier and, because we're creatures of habit, we tend to take the easier, less painful route--a route that often keeps us downtrodden in the same place, with the same people, carrying the same baggage. Often people who stay in a difficult situation, with poisonous people around them, are enablers and their relationships are laced with co-dependency issues.

We want to grow and change, but we also want our old support system to accompany us. We want to move into our new life while dragging the remnants of the old life. There is nothing new about that situation, it's just a new place with all the old fixtures. It's not a fresh start if the sour faces of ridicule and doubt come along with you. It's only a fresh start if you're aligned with support and love.

WHY WE MUST MOVE ON

We can't run and hide from a toxic situation or a poisonous person, but we can protect ourselves. Moving on doesn't have to mean that you abandon a particular relationship--it can mean that you make different choices in that relationship, to protect yourself from negative outcomes. I used to be surrounded by poison-spirited people, some people who I thought were my friends were actually members of the Mob. Once you awaken to your full potential, you get excitedly thirsty for life. You'll want to try new things, learn about this or that, and the only thing that quenches that thirst is to get to work and make the most of that newfound potential. When we fulfill our desires, we feel lovingness and kindness toward ourselves. We find appreciation for who we are, where we've been, and where we're going. We simply run out of time and grace for those who choose not to be their best selves.

Personal accolades empower us, and negative camaraderie disempowers us. You've heard the saying that negative and positive can't exist in the same realm. It's one or the other. You must make a choice and take full responsibility for which one--negative or positive--you allow to dominate your life.

It's important to know and understand that people who tread in toxicity are usually infused with a lot of fear. Underneath that fear is pain and under that pain is hurt. I know this layering from working through my own issues. These layered wounds can be deeply rooted, and some people will never work their way out of this morass. The same folks may even believe that's just who they are, but there is much more going on than what is on the surface. In no way is this process for you about making them into bad people or making you better than them. The way I characterize these negative people is only a clue to help you understand that it's difficult to allow your dreams and ideas to exist in the same space as the Mob.

In the Mob, there is no positive change happening. No one is encouraged to improve. No one is called to take on risk or explore opportunities and face the uncertainty of stepping away from the familiar.

When I have written about negative people on my website or in my newspaper column, I get a lot of passionate comments. I believe that's because so many folks are shackled to destructive people in their own lives. If negativity is not spilling over from colleagues at the office, you could very well be getting a dose of it through your television, computer screen, chance encounters in your daily routine, or even your own home. In the next chapter we'll take a closer look surviving in an often uninspiring world and how to rise above what's merely expected.

TAKING THE HIGH ROAD

This entire chapter is really about taking the high road, but I felt a need to make special mention of that concept here because sometimes taking the high road is a really challenging thing to do. If we are committed to going over and beyond where we formerly were, we must get ourselves to a higher place.

Before I took my shot at starting my own business and becoming an entrepreneur, I worked inside of newsrooms and, before that, offices and retail stores. One thing is certain: no matter the profession, the city, or the company, people have a way of being petty.

As an example, I once was leading a self-esteem program for high school girls. I was in this particular school one day a week for eight weeks, and so I began to see the same teachers week after week.

About three weeks into my work, one of the teachers began to tell me what the other teachers were saying about me, and it wasn't kind. While I was baffled that these women were belittling me while I was in the school to teach teenage girls the exact opposite behavior, I didn't let my consternation show. I listened to what the woman had to say because sometimes gossip gives us information that may help us later. However, I never spoke ill of the teachers who apparently were doing so of me. Rather than provide more ammunition to the gossip mill, I simply reminded my contact of the great job the students were doing and went on with my head up. As I went on with my work, the teachers who I was told were talking behind my back would smile in my face and I'd return the gesture, reminding myself of the high road.

You don't get a chance to make a decision to cope with disgruntled people--it is a necessary part of the spiritual transformation. Relationships with poisonous people often have good information to offer us, but the lessons aren't always apparent. Consider being a student of observation during run-ins with toxic people. Watch them trip over their hatefulness when they see that you aren't interested-- that you aren't taking the bait they're offering. Watch them try a bit harder to get you to make a snide remark. There is really nothing we can do to stop them except control how we respond. Unpleasant, messy situations will arise, but it's the approach to them that makes all the difference. The attitude that you choose to take places you on a different, higher level.

LET IT BE

A woman I once knew began spreading spiteful rumors about my husband and me. She boosted herself up on a pedestal on our backs and downplayed us with lies and childlike foolishness. Yes, there was a part of me that wanted to scream out, "hey! That's not true!" If the individuals listening to the negative banter wanted to be entertained by that lifeless nonsense, is it worth my resources and attention to defend myself to closed-minded people? As hurtful as this episode was, my husband and I chose to take the high road and let the situation be.

One thing I know for sure is that when people talk down about others, they're really expressing how they feel about themselves. They swear that life is good. You'll hear them say, "I'm so happy," or "all is great on my end." Impossible! Hatred and love--negative and positive--cannot coexist in the same realm. You can't spit venom or organize evil plots at the same time as you feel love welling up inside of you. The Universe simply doesn't work like that.

My approach to this hateful woman was, well, nothing. I didn't respond to her venomous accusations unless someone directly asked me, and then I told that inquirer the truth. Even then, I didn't go back and forth about what was or wasn't said. I took a minute or two to express the truth as I saw it. But as far as getting down on the rumor-spreading woman's level, playing in the dirt of deceit...? Nah, not interested.

People are going to choose not to like you because of how you dress, how long or short your hair is, how articulate your words are, or any of a thousand traits you have. These negative people will drum up several reasons why they don't like you, and none of those reasons have any bearings on you and the purpose you're here to serve. None of what these poisonous people say can stunt your strut unless you let it. Just let it be.

✤ STRUTTING STONES ✤

1. Who in your life doesn't mean you well? Why have you chosen to associate with him or her?

2. Is there someone in your life that you are covering for, afraid to face the truth that he/she is a negative influence in your life?

3. How much more of yourself are you willing to betray in order to please this negative person?

4. Are you truly ready to break away from this source of toxins in you life? Why or why not? What steps can you take to get ready?

5

GETTING UNHAZED

*Too many women have paved the way, taken a stand, had a voice,
and demanded respect. Don't let those gals on reality TV tell you any different.*

The average American will have spent nine years or more sitting in front of the television by the age of 65! Sounds outrageous, but it's actually the truth according to recent statistics recorded by the Nielsen Company. Can you imagine spending nine years of your life watching TV, nine precious years that we'll never get back, spent sitting infront of a screen?

We are living in the best of times: we have access to an abundance of information right at our fingertips, we can choose from hundreds of television channels, and we have our very own personal trainer on an exercise video game. We're also living in the worst of times: we have access to an abundance of information right at our fingertips, we can choose from hundreds of television channels, and we have our very own personal trainer on an exercise video game.

Depending on how we choose to use them, these opportunities can add value to our life or greatly reduce our quality of living. Our TV sets are inundated with scripted reality shows, near-nude models are plastered on magazine covers and billboards, and our beloved country is getting fatter, weaker, and broker. As a collective people, we are facing one problem after another, and we're so connected to the information highway and different forms of communication that we can't escape these problems, we can't withdraw from them. We're often glued to whatever the "talking heads" on our TV sets are selling. From slanderous political campaigns to eyelash-lengthening creams, most people are buying into the media's point of view without thinking twice about it.

Many advertisers and big companies have done a very fine job conditioning Americans to believe that one thing is better than another, without actual evidence to support their assertions. They have ingrained into our psyche that driving this car means you have class, and if you drive that other car, you don't fit in. And the thinner you are, the better looking you are, and the more opportunities you have. We've been conditioned to believe that without money, you have no power. Plenty of Hollywood and TV network executives have heavily weighed in as well; we've been tricked into expecting that bad behavior is rewarded and that the more skin you reveal, the more attention you will receive.

It's not only advertisers or executives; some celebrities and reality TV stars also bear some responsibility for these unhealthy attitudes, as well. They pull publicity stunts to stay in the public eye; they wear outlandish, skimpy attire to grab photographers' attention, and the photos that are taken slithers down into our grocery store magazine racks as venomous tabloids. Some entertainers are grinding on stage, shaking breast and buttocks in the eye of the camera. Musicians degrade women, and women degrading themselves, for a shot at fame. We are told over and over again what success, beauty, and power in today's society look like. Image after image, we're fooled into buying into an outrageous version of what our lives are supposed to mean, and, in the end, people who pursue this ideal discover that they were chasing something that can't be caught.

STRUT ICONS

Women are being misrepresented in today's media. We're lacking intelligent women, both young and old. We don't have enough graceful women in the spotlight--there are plenty of them to showcase, but according to some of the "powers that be"-a strong, polished, professional woman is not attention-grabbing enough to draw attention from the train-wreck reality show "stars". We don't have enough examples of women who are strutting their stuff--courageous women who have succeeded over difficult circumstances and are still graceful trailblazers. We need to see more women who are proud of their natural beauty and who choose to celebrate life according to their own beat.

I'd like to see a reality show based on a woman like international fashion designer and businesswoman Diane von Furstenberg. I have yet to see a strong, confident female lead a show that chronicles the daily workings in her world, and she would be a great choice for this role. This iconic and charismatic 65-year-old invented the wrap dress and based on her personal views on life and professional accolades, she appears to be comfortable in the skin she's in. I've never heard talk of a show starring her, but it would be great to see this powerhouse woman living authentically, without the unproductive cat-fights and malicious put-downs so prevalent in current female-centered TV shows. It would be so rewarding to see a woman embrace her age, looks, past hardships, and life without any apologies or any attempts to mimic or become someone else.

"The best way to age is to be involved and engage in the world, and to assume the person that you are. Your age, your country, your social background--it doesn't matter," Diane von Furstenberg said. She's letting nature take its course and explained that she decided not to alter her appearance as she ages. She is quoted as saying, "at the end it's all about being your own best friend and liking yourself. Life is a journey and landscapes change and people come and go, but you are always there."

And von Furstenberg really sums it up. We should be friendly with ourselves and accept what comes our way in life, including relationships and an aging body. But it's such a challenge when we're faced with so many distractions and drama being shoved at us by the entertainment and news media. How do we override the system and make sure that we're not being sucked into the unhealthy mindset being promoted to us? How do we decipher what's purely entertainment and what's real? How can we teach our children and young women that what's constantly portrayed in the movies and online doesn't reflect the reality of authentic, normal life?

Very carefully and very consciously--that's how we will manage to separate ourselves from the overindulgence in too much greed, scandal, crime, pornography, texting, and all the other media distractions flying at us. We've got to guard ourselves with consciousness and take confidence in knowing who we are, so that we don't compare ourselves with others. We've got to know facts and guard ourselves with information, and we need to know when and how to unplug. If we can't concisely manage ourselves, then we are unconsciously giving a true beast access to us and dominion over us. I don't believe we truly want to sell ourselves out to that avalanche of loose values and fast lifestyles that permeates our media. I can't imagine that we would really want to become zombiefied by all the unreal-reality hype or scripted movies that use violence, oversexualization, and vulgarity to provide us pointless and value-less entertainment.

LACK AND ATTACK

While reporting in Dallas, I had an incredible opportunity to interview a woman I've admired and celebrated since I was a teenager. The first time I read the book "I Know Why the Caged Bird Sings", I knew I would someday thank the author, Dr. Maya Angelou, for that story. Nearly two decades later, that opportunity beautifully unfolded for me.

This was not an easy interview to get, for two reasons. One, the producer didn't see civil rights activist and best-selling author Dr. Angelou newsworthy in the grand scheme of things. Two, I also had to do some convincing of Dr. Angelou's camp because she was stepping back from granting most media interviews.

Dr. Angelou was speaking at the University of Texas at Arlington (UTA) and while it wasn't breaking news, I found her presence there to be relevant to women's issues as well as societal concerns. I wrote a heartfelt, truthful letter to her, detailing why I felt her voice could be used in a positive way through a presence on local TV news during her visit. For weeks, I heard nothing, and I began to despair. Suddenly, the day before her trip to Texas, I got the phone call that we were on!

I quickly swapped schedules with another reporter--since the producer didn't want this story I decided to do it on my own time. I worked the 3 a.m. shift the night before, and then headed out to the UTA's campus to meet Dr. Angelou once I got off work. I was also fortunate to have a cameraman who knew my passion and agreed to help me on his day off, as a favor. Before I knew it, I was sitting with this incredible living legend talking about everything from worldly affairs to spiritual growth.

I asked Dr. Angelou about women and our desire to compete in today's rugged, fast-paced world. I asked her how we measure up when it seems like there are so many things stacked against us and her face grew very concerned. She firmly stated, "you mustn't compare yourself to others, all comparisons are ominous. He or she will always be taller, thinner, better-looking, better-educated, or just better at this or that." She paused and looked gently at me and explained, "all you can do is be the best Raquel you know how to be. That's all any of us can do, is be the best we know how to be."

I heard Dr. Angelou in that moment and I clearly understood her point of view. After all, this was a woman speaking from great experience. Her attitude is powerful yet humble. This is a woman who faced enormous challenges as a child and young woman, but continued on to pave the way for other women as she herself grew and succeeded. During my time with her, it was obvious that she did a lot of her work for the women who would one day stand on her shoulders. She pushed the envelope for civil rights issues--not so much to make things better for herself, but for the millions of faceless women who would have it a bit easier and perhaps better because of her efforts.

So, when Dr. Angelou talked with me about comparisons, I took it seriously because I was one of those women who sometimes compared myself to others, and in turn would find something that I thought was lacking in me, I was attacking myself by those senseless comparisons. She was right, the person you're comparing yourself to always ends up being better than you in some way. Our minds make them better, no matter the reality of their own situations.

I will never be anyone other than who I am, end of story. All I can be is the best Raquel. I noticed that, when I finally let go of my urge to compare myself to a girl in a magazine or a wealthy colleague, I was gentler with myself. I could see my own beauty in a different way. When I shut down that voice of comparisons in my head, a space was created. In that space, I instead planted affirmations of acceptance and kindheartedness toward myself.

Most of us were teased about one thing or another, from grade school on through college. That constant negative input from others can really hurt our self-esteem, especially when we see perfect images of others and their lives splashed around our society. These images aren't real. These people don't really live the way they are portrayed to others. I suppose that if you and I had a make-up team, a personal chef, a personal trainer, an expert photographer, a hairdresser or weave/wig specialist, a fan blowing our hair on a professionally arranged set, and a $20,000 photo shoot fee, we'd look refreshed and happy, too!

DRAW YOUR OWN CONCLUSIONS

Researchers have long recognized and warned that too much television or time on the web isn't good for us. In recent years, however, scientists have taken a closer look at our technological habits and this new information about how much our media addiction is costing us is terrifying news.

"The computer is like electronic cocaine," says Peter Whybrow, the director of the Semel Institute for Neuroscience and Human Behavior at UCLA. Some people are addicted to the Internet and often experience sensations of hyper-energy when using online media, this euphoric feeling is followed by bouts of depression. Doctors have noted that people who are frequent users of the Internet have the same brain scan characteristics during online activity as drug addicts exhibit during a high.

Most of us have become reliant upon our computers, cell phones, and Internet. I know that, while researching a project, I can jump online twenty or thirty separate times a day, not including checking emails, connecting to friends through social sites, or updating my own website. I can see how easy it is to become addicted to using the Internet, and I believe we're just seeing the beginning of a much more serious problem on that front.

In my home, we have rules in place for all of this technology. One of our rules is that there is no TV, computer, or cell phone use until after morning prayer/meditation. I also have budgeted my time allowed for social sites and emails. I avoid the "Watch This Video Now" buttons because one click leads to another and--before you know it--forty-five minutes have passed and you have nothing to show for the time.

To really manage your time on the web, you might want to

consider various productivity tools such as LeechBlock, a free program that allows you to block time-wasting websites.

Putting boundaries around electronic forms of communication helps to keep us alert to the world around us. We're hearing the term "dumbing down" a lot, especially with reference to young adults. While this is a bothersome phrase because of the inherent insult, it's true. People are losing the ability to speak well because they're typing most of their communication. Spelling and grammar skills are plummeting. Many of us aren't able to form critical thoughts when faced with basic problems. I believe these difficulties with fundamental communications skills are at least propagated, if not actually caused, by the pervasive presence and use of electronic media in contemporary life.

We're losing a lot of the vital communication skills we learned early on, but what this digital drama is also stealing is our ability to connect well with each other and with ourselves. During my work on self-improvement topics with teens and young adults, I have noticed that my students' ability to socialize and relate to one another is much worse than when I was that age. Some of these young people don't have much expression or feeling in the way they relate to others. For example, while I was leading a public speaking class at a charter school in Cleveland, Ohio, one of my students turned in a term paper with the first paragraph structured conventionally, and then he began writing in "text speak", with many abbreviations, misspellings, and other non-standard English.

Maybe this is the way the world is going. Perhaps the current online revolution will also transform the English language. What really concerns me here, though, is the great divide that the constant incomplete and impersonal communications cause in our spirits. We are not mechanical, we're spiritual beings with certain needs and wants. A computer or TV show will never be able to fill that need. One of our mandatory needs as a human being is to have contact and connection with others. We need to feel the expressions of love and joy, peace and sorrow. We were built to feel the experience of life, and a computer just can't give us that raw emotion or attention so naturally required. An email is not the same as a hug. An "LOL" text message is a poor substitute for hearing a friend's belly laugh on the phone or in person.

Consider putting a halt to your use with some media and technologies as you become tuned to your own thoughts and what's really happening in the world. Look through your own perspective and arrive at your own thoughts instead of allowing fast-moving commercials and lowbrow movies to think for you.

CHANGE THE CHANNEL

For the most part, when we're soaking in our favorite television programs, our active thought process is resting, but our brains are still busy. We're picking up on messages in the programming without really thinking about them, and a lot of the big business media companies and advertisers are very aware of this.

Once you clear your head and get straight on who is really controlling your life, the hidden messages in some printed ads, commercials, and reality shows are easier to spot than a pig in a blanket. With mindful viewing, you can just see these bids for your approval for what they are. You will be able to bypass these manipulated images of hype and perfection by asking yourself one question: does this movie/product/article add value to my life? In other words, does this media I am consuming enrich my life in any way, or is it just a waste of time, energy, and brainpower?

With this one simple question, you're able to make wise decisions and feel good about the choices you're making involving your place in the world and the information that you allow into your mind. Living a spiritual, enlightened life takes all the support you can get, and controlling this mass medium will greatly serve your quest. The things that you feed to your mind and spirit are just as important as what you feed your body.

I enjoy the pastimes of TV viewing and Internet surfing as a way to unwind and obtain information, but I choose the programs I watch and web sites I visit based on that question of value. There are some programs that help me learn about cooking and entertaining, while others make me laugh or encourage my search for living stronger. Entertainment is entertainment; it's not the gospel or a guide to how we should govern our lives. People would be much better off if they knew how to put the messages constantly thrown at them into proper perspective.

WHAT THEY WON'T TELL YOU

Most television executives, advertisers, and Hollywood moviemakers are in the industry to make money, not to be our role models or make the world better and safer. We can't blame them for running a business. I mean, after all, they are just responding to what viewers want. They're following what's popular and what brings masses of people to their product or service.

What you may not know is just how much of an effort companies are putting up to attract our attention. We're not talking about basic money in marketing campaigns, we're subject to a very aggressive approach to reach beyond you and me--they're going after the kids.

According to one national news report, in 1980 companies spent about $100 million marketing to kids. Today, they're spending nearly $17 billion annually.

This effort to market toward children isn't new, companies have been at it for a long time. Some advertisers have purposely planted images and ideas into children's minds, hoping to gain their loyalty as a life-long customer. All kids grow up, and if they're exposed to over twenty thousand thirty-second TV commercials per year throughout their childhoods, as statistics currently show, then it's very likely that some of that input is going to stick in those little minds.

I grew up wanting to have that toilet paper that the funny guy in the glasses didn't want people to squeeze. When I was a kid, I felt bad that my family couldn't afford what I regarded as luxurious bathroom tissue. Seeing that man protect it like it was some precious thing made a mark on me. I thought that this brand of toilet paper was so precious, it was meant only for special people. In my house we had generic toilet paper. I don't know what that company's intention was behind the commercial but watching it as a kid, I took on that interpretation and the feeling that we weren't "good enough" for the "squeezable" toilet paper stuck with me for years.

Today's commercial messages are way more aggressive than the nice man in the supermarket clinging to soft rolls of bathroom tissue. We are all getting blasted with messages that can be overwhelming to the brain.

International spiritual teacher and best selling author Eckhart Tolle says in his book "A New Earth" that overindulgence in television watching isn't good for anyone, but that we all should be especially cautious of programs that he says makes us unconscious. "Avoid watching programs and commercials that assault you with rapid succession of images that change every two or three seconds or less," is Mr. Tolle's advice. He says that watching too much of the tube contributes to Attention Deficit Disorder and other mental problems, which can all wreak havoc on our relationships, work, and overall well-being.

Just as the executives of those television shows make a decision on what they choose to pass on to us, you and I must make an executive decision on what we allow to be passed on to us. We don't need the guilt of a television program, commercial, TV news broadcast, or web site telling us that we're smart if we drive this car, we're sexy if we wear that dress, or we're pretty if we use this beauty product. We don't need a talking head to tell us which political candidate is the right choice for us or what song we should be singing. We've got to use our own brains, do our own research, and selectively withdraw from the often hypnotizing state of much of the programming to which we're exposed.

PAULA DEEN

She's one of the most popular and charismatic chefs in the world and has sold millions of cookbooks. Paula Deen has built an empire based around her love for family and having fun in the kitchen. She has been criticized in the past for sharing some not-so-healthy recipes on her cooking shows. Critics denounced some of Deen's hearty meals because of some of the high-fat and high-calorie ingredients. Deen responded to those critics by saying that her goal was to help Americans make tasty food that fit into their budgets.

The plot thickened in early 2012 when Deen announced that she was diabetic and was committed to getting healthier through a change in her diet. She stated that she wanted to share healthier recipes with fans as well. Later that summer, she was featured in a cover article in People Magazine, showing off some new recipes and sporting a new body, minus 30 pounds.

I was happy for Deen's weight loss success and I posted the article on a social media website. The reviews were mixed, but what was shocking to me was that some people were actually annoyed with Deen for losing the weight. I received comments from people who thought that she betrayed them. Some suggested that Deen had made some people fat by way of her cooking show and now that she's taking on a healthier perspective, she's leaving behind the fans that ate themselves into health problems.

Paula Deen didn't make anyone fat. She didn't force people to make her recipes, she didn't force anyone to eat the food, and she certainly didn't strap her viewers down to prevent them from exercising.

For as much as we see in our media, we can't blame electronic inputs for our own personal problems or missteps. If we consciously--or even unconsciously--buy into an idea, advice, or product, it's not the responsibility of the TV network, the reality stars, or the inventors behind our digital conveniences. It is our responsibility to get sound information and make responsible choices that empower us.

✻ STRUTTING STONES ✻

1. At some time or another most of us have wished for a body or face or life like a character on TV or an entertainer, without realizing that we may have been magnifying that person's image while diminishing our own beauty or accomplishments. Can you

recall a time that you may have felt "less than" or inferior based on the perceptions viewed in media? Recount the emotions that stirred up in you and how did it make you feel about yourself?

2. When you compare yourself to others, what does it cost you, what do you loose in the process?

3. Do you need to make some changes in how much time you're spending watching television or surfing the Internet? Most of us could use a little "media diet" in our lives. What two things can you do to better control and monitor how much time you spend in such passive pursuits?

1.

2.

(Remember, by the age of 65 most Americans will have spent nearly 10 years of their lives watching TV--what do they have to show for that time?)

4. What TV programs, movies, or websites add value to your life and inspire you to be your absolute best? How do they help you to improve?

5. Get rid of all the empty media baggage and free up some space in your mind for other, more positive content. Erase old numbers out of your cell phone directory. If you are no longer in contact with certain people or the friendship has ended, let them go. Check your email account to see if you are hanging on to any disempowering emails that are not serving your higher purpose. If you have any DVD's or books that aren't in alignment with your values, trade them in or give them away. Don't let mindless media hobble your strut!

Part Two
Self ReNew

6

PURPOSEFUL LIVING

*"One needs something to believe in, something for which one can
have whole-hearted enthusiasm. One needs to feel that one's life
has meaning, that one is needed in this world."*
~ Hannah Senesh

Living a life of purpose has a lot to do with using the talents and abilities you were born with, the things you love to do, the things that you can do naturally, effortlessly, those little things and big things that doesn't identify with the word "work".

A key to unlocking purpose is clarity, you must get clear on what you really want, not what everyone else wants for you, but what you want and why. Very often we can't find our purpose because it's clouded by unidentified truths and unsolicited advice, 1980's baggage and faked experiences- that is we can't see what we really want because we're too busy facing what we don't want.

It is really as simple as asking, "What do I want" and letting the answers flow. Do this with an dissatisfying career, relationships, your health or other areas and you might be surprise to see that the very things you say you don't want are right there in your face and in your space. Take your energy off what you don't want and focus solely on one question: What do I want?

YOUR TIME IS YOUR TIME

When I was 25, it bugged me to hear a 19-year-old declare that he knew his passion early in life and that's why he's loving his work and making a good living at it. When I was 31, I felt foolish hearing about the 21-year-old girl who left college to pursue her dream, and is now running a business. I couldn't understand why some people could find both passion and purpose so early in life, as I felt further and further away from my own true calling. Then I got into my mid-thirties and by then, all I could think was, "this is ridiculous!" I became so frustrated with myself for not only living off-purpose but for--at that time--not even being able to truly identify what I was meant to do.

Through this work of transforming thoughts and getting back to my spirit, one of the first things I did was release the habitual cycle of comparing my life and timelines to other people. Everyone has a different situation and a different set of circumstances, so we're not going to all be in the game together, some of us are spectators for a little while before we dive into the game. Some people grab hold of a piano at the age of six and they never let it go, others find their way by bumping into something else that pulls out their hidden talents and abilities. We all have something in us that has to come out. We all have something that we're supposed to share with others. That sharing might mean within your household, community, country, or world. It could be more than just one purpose, it could be many.

Once I went through a self-review and careful examination of my life, I clearly reconnected with what I feel was one of the purposes for my life. I was relieved to see that God didn't forget me, that He did in fact have something special for me to do. I realized that He actually showed me those signs very early, but I somehow got off-track.

DETACHMENT FROM PURPOSE

When I was a kid, I loved telling stories, writing them, and even speaking them. I also loved to speak before crowds of people. Public speeches didn't frighten me at all, in fact, I stretched out most of my speaking opportunities because I liked talking to people. I picked up on facial expressions very early and when someone gave me a look of surprise or delight, I'd work harder to get another one.

I guess I was maybe eight years old when I sat in my bedroom and recorded my new speaking and acting skills. I still have the original cassette tape recording of me playing a preacher woman on one side and acting out a monologue of "All My Children" star Erica Kane on the other side. In my role as Erica, I was smooching it up with some invisible man named Tom and crying over his miserable self. But the preaching side was moving, with heart-felt inflection in my voice and profound thoughts about Jesus and living right. In between all of the faux-crying over the soap-opera drama and interruptions from my mother calling me to come wash the dishes was a kid who was telling the world then that she wanted to be of service.

In my early teens, I pitched a proposal to a neighborhood community center, The Friendly House, hoping to teach dance classes to children. The director of the center loved my idea. I took what I had learned from my own previous dance classes and recitals and transformed my knowledge into lessons that I could now teach. When I was fifteen years old I produced my very first production, a talent show called "Boogie Night". Tickets were $3.00 and the small community auditorium was sold out. This was a chance for the kids I was instructing to show off their new skills. Midway through the event, some kids started fighting and closed down the show, but it made a few hundred dollars for the community center and gave my students something to feel good about. My involvement with this production also gave me a sense of something that I couldn't name at the time, but today I call it a sense of self.

Somewhere along the way, I abandoned my teaching vocation and love for producing events and got on a different track, which took me to other interests. Because I also loved to write and share with others, I thought a job in local TV news broadcasting was a good fit, but I wasn't aware of the many other duties of the job that turned out to be wrong for me. So, my involvement with broadcasting appeared to be a wrong turn but I now know that it was the perfect turn for me. Perhaps I needed to find a different format of broadcasting, but I was able to learn an extraordinary amount about my values, principles and humanity and these lessons have a tremendous impact on my work today.

My time in broadcasting wasn't wasteful at all. Sometimes we might feel disconnected from our purpose based on the decisions we've made. We might feel like we're a million miles away from where we should be, but perhaps we are right where we need to be. How do you know you're not being groomed for something greater right now? Maybe you're stuck in a place that you despise, but this experience is preparing you to go into your passion with humility and a greater understanding of who you are.

If I had been given a million dollars at the age of twenty-five or even thirty, I would've squandered it. I wasn't emotionally mature to handle that much money responsibly. I had not learned enough about myself and how life works to do the right thing with that amount of money. At twenty-five or thirty, I hadn't experienced enough to develop a women's conference, write a weekly newspaper column, or write this book. No one wants to read about anger, sadness, confusion, or pity, but that's what my younger, inexperienced self would have portrayed.

Rest assured that, if you haven't seen it already, your purpose is still in you.

IT'S CLOSER THAN YOUR BREATH

While I didn't connect with the workings of local media during my time in broadcasting, I did find great fulfillment in the community service part of my job. When Hurricane Katrina hit New Orleans, many evacuees landed in Dallas, which paved the way for some incredible stories about strength, courage, and faith. This need of others also brought out the goodness in others, as people in Dallas and across the country opened their pocketbooks and their hearts. Working during that time was stressful because so many people were suffering and panicking. These evacuees had lost everything, but I felt a great sense of responsibility of relating their true experience to the masses. I've often prayed and asked God to use me as a vessel. In this instance, I felt that is exactly what happened. While I had many gripes about what was actually "news" and how it was covered, my work during this ordeal was, I believe, part of my purpose.

I also received calls to emcee events or speak at fundraisers, which is where I really felt passion rise up within me. This work was all volunteer (unpaid), but I didn't care. I found myself on the stage at University of North Texas (UNT), facilitating a symposium with Yolanda King shortly after the passing of her mother, Coretta Scott King. I was able to sit with the eldest daughter of Rev. Dr. Martin Luther King, Jr. and interview her in front of a live audience. I felt vibrant and honored to be in that space, sharing a wonderful, thought-provoking experience with so many other like-minded learners.

Life isn't rosy all the time. You may not always get what you want or find all the answers right when and where you think you need them. You may not feel like you're on purpose one hundred percent of the time--or even fifty percent, sometimes. Your lustrous moments of inspiration might just be a few minutes out of your day, but through those little windows, you'll be able to get the bigger picture of what it would feel like to live with passion and purpose every day. You can use these tiny moments as inspiration and fuel to keep searching and creating ways to get to the work you love on a full-time basis. Most of my news career was spent chasing down crime and weather stories-- that was neither my passion nor my big purpose in life. Because I was able to work with the community in a different capacity, I was able to hold onto the truth of knowing that I would someday lead a life and seek experiences that fulfilled the person I was truly meant to be. Your purpose is always close to you, it's with you right now, closer than you might know.

ALWAYS BE TRUE TO YOU

At one time in my life, I was working hard at the wrong thing, trying to be someone who I wasn't, and that pretense brought on a lot of stress and pressure. As if the tight deadlines of live television weren't enough, try meeting those demands while measuring yourself against your peers and always finding yourself, as Dr. Angelou said, "falling short".

On one particular job, I had a really terrific supervisor "Gary" who he really took a chance on me when he hired me. I didn't have as much experience as some of the other applicants, but I sure did want to learn under his direction. During my job interview, I was one hundred percent genuine and expressed high enthusiasm for working under his leadership. Once I had been hired, I began to realize the office politics and how respected some reporters were, I wanted to grow my career to another level--to become one of those reporters. Somehow I got the idea that I needed to become someone else, someone who wasn't me, in order to do it. (I would later understand how I arrived at this thought through the work I shared in Chapter 2 Patterns/Emotions Figure 1 &2.)

So I tried hard to prove myself to Gary, only this time I didn't make a recurring role as myself. Instead, at times I played the role of a "reporter". Or, more precisely, who I believed a "reporter" would be. I battled with this pretense and with the fact that I was tangled in a career where I felt I had to lower myself by relinquishing the morals and values that had been important to me.

I thought my supervisor would appreciate my efforts and recognize my ability to "play big" in the newsroom, but when I decided that the "star reporter" role wasn't for me, that I had no interest in chasing down the worst thing that happened in our world overnight and follow gloomy accounts for a 8-10 hour shift, I felt as if I failed myself as well as Gary, who had given me the chance to build up what I thought would become a promising career. Gary was such a kind, generous person to me and the last thing I wanted to do was disappoint him. In the end, I really believed that I had let him down. I never became the type of reporter he wanted--or so I thought.

It would be years later before I found out how wrong I was. Luckily, I'd kept the lines of communication open with Gary and there came a time when I asked him for a letter of reference for another news job that I thought would offer me a partial platform for the type of enterprising news I was interested in. He didn't waste a minute responding to my request. He quickly drafted a great letter and let me know that he supported my decision to move forward in the news business.

When I read that letter, I finally understood why this insightful man had hired me in the first place. As he wrote in the letter, "Raquel was one of approximately two hundred applicants for the position. After she interviewed with us, she rose above all others because of her passion and her heart. It was an easy decision to hire Raquel." Wow. What a great thing to learn about oneself! In the recommendation letter, he went on to explain why.

"During her interview and later when we worked together, Raquel displayed qualities unlike many of her peers," Gary said. "The news business has a tendency to 'harden' reporters. It can numb some of life's hurt and pain. The TV news business never hardened Raquel to painful things she witnessed as a professional journalist. It had just the opposite effect. It ignited a deep sense of compassion."

When I got this letter I wept. Everything had come full-circle for me. There I had been, in a business where yes, many of my colleagues were hardened by the many tragedies happening in the world. I couldn't understand their insensitivities because I was operating from a different place, but, in trying to become like them, I was losing myself.

All along, this supervisor didn't hire me to become like the employees he already had, he hired me to bring a different element to his team. I nearly ruined his choice with my own thoughts and assumptions, my own image of what a top reporter should be. I thought he was expecting another hard-hitting, crime-chasing reporter, and I tried to become that person, as my old thinking patterns were telling me to be. What he wanted instead was the best of what Raquel had to offer.

SHIFTING GEARS

Thomas Kuhn, an accredited scientist and--some would say-- a philosopher, changed the game when he popularized the term "paradigm shift" (a radical change in underlying beliefs or theory). Dr. Kuhn, a Ph.D. physicist trained at Harvard University, has made many discoveries in his research, but none prompted more attention than a controversial claim in his 1962 book, "The Structure of Scientific Revolutions".

In his book, Dr. Kuhn suggested that scientists were not objective or independent thinkers, as most people assumed. Kuhn explained that most scientists are puzzle-solvers who aim to confirm what they already know, rather than discover new knowledge, particularly if the new information contradicts information they already hold.

This wasn't a popular statement by Dr. Kuhn, who weathered a lot of criticism from colleagues all over the world after his book came out. However, he pressed on with his theory and called for a change in how problems should be approached in the scientific world. Essentially, he was advocating a change in the thinking of the great minds of science. He wanted these leading researchers to develop the ability to shift thought patterns and look at the same inputs as before, but now see something different.

Today, we can see a paradigm shift with the computer, which provides one of the biggest shifts of our time. Computers started out as simple word processors, but have evolved into a global phenomenon, which allows us to connect, see, share, and work worldwide in an instant.

You have the capability of looking at the same thing and seeing something else, too. In regards to your purpose, you can shift your thinking and find all sorts of clues and evidence telling you why your life has meaning and what you can do to enforce and explore that meaning.

Last month, what did your future look like? Take into account the old feelings and beliefs that may have been hindering your growth in the past. Perhaps now, after working through the exercises in this book, you can take off your blinders. What if you took all those flashes of influence in your mind, all those low- and high-points, and transferred them into a ball of usable motivation to proceed with passion, confirm your purpose, and strengthen your life? What then?

↟ STRUTTING STONES ↟

1. Was there ever something you heard or saw as a kid and the minute you did, you knew it was for you? What thing(s) sparked your attention when you were a kid or teenager? What was so significant about it and how did it make you feel?

2. Did you ever see someone's eyes light up when you performed a particular talent or showed ability in something? Write as much as you can about that experience, about how you felt and how you can recapture that ability.

3. Quickly, without giving it contemplation but only operating from first impressions, write down a time you felt like you were detached from your purpose. Were there lessons learned through that experience that greatly served you later in life?

Give three examples of improvement from such "course corrections".

1.

2.

3.

4. List 5 genuine qualities that you admire about yourself and write a short promise to yourself of how you'll always remain true to these qualities.

1.

2.

3.

4.

5.

5. What situation in your life right now needs a paradigm shift?

Take another look at this issue/problem and ask yourself a few
questions:

- What's the best thing about this situation?

- What am I learning through this situation?

- It won't always be this way, but while it is, what's something
  new or different that I can bring to this situation to get a
  different outcome or response?

6. Make a list of several current obstacles in your life, and next to
   each one of them list a strengthening element of the situation.
   Use the strengths of your stumbles. Repackage all of the things
   that have brought you to where you are today and transfer those
   experiences to inform your quest toward living a purposeful life.
   Don't let your back-story go to waste, use it to build a new
   story--a new, strong, courageous story.

7

BEING UNREASONABLE & UNAVAILABLE

"There are no good girls gone wrong--just bad girls found out." – Mae West

Something in you is moving. You're climbing out of a challenging situation or climbing toward a better situation, but either way, you're on the move. Something is commanding you to keep going, to stay on track. That same voice is also in need of your immediate attention. It might be time for you to sit still, get ready, and put some outside efforts on hold for the time being.

There are times in life where we just need to scale back and stop being everything to everybody. We can't save the world and we can't check everything off our to-do list every single time. We need a break and we need to let others know that we're checking out just for a little while--taking some attention away from the things that don't need our watchful eye or perfect attention. Becoming unreasonable and unavailable is simply about shutting down your 24-hour "Open for Business" service and putting a "In Championship Training--Will Return When Good and Ready" sign up instead.

If you want your life to work, be willing to make it work and that means putting things in place that benefit your overall well being. You've got to monitor it and make the necessary tweaks and repairs needed, part of the doing in this work calls for focus and a strong commitment to yourself. You are in complete giving mode during this "check-out", only this time, you're giving to yourself. Another way to look at it is like a recovery process--you're the patient, the doctor, and the rehab therapist all wrapped up in one. You don't need to apologize to anyone for granting your resources upon yourself.

As "the patient" heals and strongly recovers, there's going to be some therapy needed. That means putting a lid on the demands placed on you, it means declining the requests you're really not interested in, and it means sticking to "no" when you say it.

Before I go any further, let me state the obvious. Few of us are able to totally unplug from the world for three days, three weeks, or three months while we realign ourselves. So, for the sake of speaking realistically, I'm not suggesting that you ignore your responsibilities and cut off communication with those who need you. Nor am I suggesting that anyone become arrogant in taking necessary time for themselves. What I will suggest is stepping back from your life and noticing where you keep tossing yourself into another activity or someone else's needs, Notice how much time and energy you have remaining for yourself.

For greater understanding, we can look to any athlete who has excelled in their sport. While in training, they shut down the outside world and unplug from anything and anyone who will distract them from their goals. They become unreasonable and unavailable because they know what's at stake and the cost of winning. They're certainly not like this one hundred percent of the time, but when it's time to go after a championship, everything changes for them.

Regaining your strut is one of your championships. It may not be a win for the fans, it's much more personal than that. A victory in this arena is one on the most sacred of levels, very intimate and very revealing.

If you decide to change things up and shut down the revolving door in your life, you will create a level of awareness that will help you to see things differently. You will feel a depth that you haven't felt in years, if ever. Freeing up time to do what you want to do is like treating yourself to a favorite candy--it makes the world seem sweeter. You feel better while you're eating it--you savor it and enjoy it. You are worth every bit of sweetness you can get your hands on. If that treat actually is candy or ice cream, that's great. However, I was speaking more of the sweetness in the doing, the taking time for you. Whether it's a weekend walk through the woods, an early morning devotion or journaling session, or a midweek evening yoga class, go into the event with you on your mind and in your focus.

I'd like to ask you to consider getting tough on all of the demands on your time and attention. I'm going to ask you to give some of these commitments up with the intention of giving instead to yourself. Are you open to that?

POTTY IN THE BUCKET

When I told my husband the name of this subsection he looked at me and said, "You're not really going to call it that, are you?"

I responded, "Yes, I'll call it as it is." And I then quickly reminded him that I was five years old at the time. So again, I'll make another reminder--I was only a 5-year-old at the time.

I grew up in a five-bedroom house with one bathroom and sometimes there were five to eight people living there, which was torture on a little girl's bladder. When adults had the coveted throne, they took their old sweet time. I guess they figured since we were just kids, our bladders were stronger.

My cousins bought into it. They would jump around, cross their legs, squeeze their hands, and even grit their teeth to hold in that urge to urinate. I wasn't into that game. It didn't make a bit of sense to me to go through such agony to do something that my body needed to naturally do. I didn't like punishing myself because of the slowness of someone else, so I knew I had to figure out a way to release it. So, through my inquisitive and somewhat imaginative mind, I invented a half bath outside in our backyard.

An old five-gallon bucket became my emergency bathroom. I peed in that bucket whenever the main room was occupied--during the morning, at night, it didn't matter. After using the bucket, I flushed it clean with the water from a garden hose and dumped the liquid in the back alley. No one knew how I was able to hold my water for so long, and I never told. I'm sure when my mother reads this section, she'll have a few questions and laughs for me!

In peeing in the bucket, I did what I had to do. I was too young to make the emotional connection at the time, but what I was tending to was a need. I was avoiding the aggravation and sometimes pain of holding my urine in repeatedly for no good reason. I was, even at that young age, trying to figure out how to take care of myself when the traditional approach wasn't available.

Isn't it a sheer joy to know that our younger selves had such a powerful instinct? The part of us that hadn't yet been introduced to the limitations of the world, that hadn't experienced so much cruelty yet. As kids, we all have strong instincts. We knew how to do things for ourselves and we did them without fear. We managed ourselves effortlessly.

Taking care of yourself or putting yourself first isn't selfish as in the standard definition. It is, however, selfish in a kindhearted, self-love type of way. Tending to your needs isn't arrogant, it's authentic, but it's also a hard dose to accept for so many women. We can look to the older women in our families and neighborhoods, when they become empty nesters. So many of them don't know what to do, they feel lonely and frightened. They don't really know how to embrace this new time for themselves because they've been giving to, and caring for, others for years. They've been the mom, chauffeur, cook, tutor, employee, colleague, business owner, home executive, maid, wife, sister, friend, aunt, and daughter. Trying to give to everyone in those roles for five, ten, even thirty years creates a separation within us. We feel pulled apart, down-trodden, and disconnected.

We're not that five-year old girl with a full bladder, but we do have needs that are just as relevant and important. If one of your desires is to make a great impact in your family or work, then get yourself rooted in your center. Find some balance that's got your name on it and retreat to that whenever you need to.

SPEAK UP...RIGHT NOW

You're probably familiar with the self-help saying borrowed from flight attendants' instructions--put your oxygen mask on first, which means taking care of yourself first, so that you can take care of others.

It is in our nature, our genetic makeup to be concerned about others first. It's our human conditioning to do, and we feel bad when we don't tend to others first. I'm not sure when we adopted this thought process--perhaps somewhere in between our great-great-great-grandmothers and our mothers, there was a separation in thought, the wires got twisted. Women abandoned themselves for the sake of caring for others, or maybe they never did learn to put themselves first. Maybe that wasn't even an option for these foremothers.

That informative airplane safety tip has been used many times over in recent years, and I believe the concept is making headway with millions of women. I believe more and more women are becoming more comfortable with tending to their needs. More are speaking up and speaking out. Many are finding it empowering to stand up and say what needs to be said, but there is still a huge void in our confidence and ability to speak up for ourselves.

Somehow our thoughts and feelings get trampled on. We let the small offenses go and the big ones go with them, too. Some of us drag our feet in defending ourselves but it usually comes down to how we feel about ourselves. We remained tight-lipped because maybe we're afraid no one will listen, it'll draw to much attention our way, or we don't want to cause trouble. What's really lurking under those excuses for you? How are you feeling about yourself when you decide to bite your tongue on issues or problems that need your input?

We can often find ourselves inconvenienced by the activity of someone else. We might make certain allowances because it's a kid or because everyone is rushing, or because it's raining--these are just a few of the little white lies we hide behind when we are fearful of speaking up. We can find all sorts of reasons why we shouldn't say something, when it only takes one reason to say it: "I am worth it."

If the issue at hand is important to you, voicing it is the only way to take action. Nipping it in the bud is the only way to keep your conscience clear because, no matter what happens as a result of your asking, you at least put yourself first and you spoke up and said what needed to be said.

At times, I still struggle with meeting my own needs first, but I'm much better than when I started. I've grown from the times when I have spoken up for myself. What's really comforting about this process is the feeling when it's over that you have cared for yourself. When my gut sends me a message of discomfort, I have to honor that, and if the situation is something that warrants my attention, I have to speak up.

A few years ago, I was on an airplane returning home after a grueling week of leadership training. All I could think about doing was sleeping through the three-hour flight. I nestled into my window seat and covered up and then the seat started shaking.

A little five- or six-year-old girl in the row behind me began kicking my seat--not tapping it, but kicking it. I figured her mother would stop her soon, since most adults are aware of how annoying this can be. The mother kept talking to the little girl as if nothing were happening.

I began to have a conversation with myself that seemed more like a battle, "should I say something?" "Oh, she's just a kid." "They purchased tickets, just like I did, so they can do whatever they want." I suddenly came to my senses and reminded myself to ask for what I need and do it now.

I calmly turned around and spoke directly to the mother, "could you please ask your daughter to stop kicking the chair? I'm trying to rest." The look this woman gave me was not at all pleasant and, at that point, I frankly didn't care. I wasn't asking her to muzzle the little girl, just stop her from kicking my seatback. The kicking soon stopped and I was proud of myself for handling it politely, regardless of the sneering look the mother gave me.

Most of the time, I sincerely believe that people understand what you need. If you convey your message with tact and grace, you'll feel a lot better for speaking your piece- so you can have peace. And, even in the times when you don't get what you want, at least you asked. You spoke up and that engenders esteem, adding one more golden egg to your power basket.

BUILDING BOUNDARIES

People will certainly cross the line with you. If you don't have a definite line drawn, those poisonous others will disrespect you over and over again. If you don't have clear boundaries, they'll ignore your viewpoint and disregard your stance. We must teach people how to treat us. You can model the exact behavior you expect from others by how you treat yourself. When it comes to establishing personal boundaries, lip service is a bunch of hot air. Your actions are what set the pace and those actions can change the game enormously!

Verbalizing your boundary list doesn't work. You can't go up to someone and say, "all right, I have new boundaries and I want you to respect them, here they are." Adults are much like kids, they don't do what we say, and they do what they see us do. They follow how we treat ourselves and how they see others treating us.

Setting personal boundaries and putting them into action are two very different missions. Executing each one of these steps is crucial to gaining momentum in your strut, because the treatment we accept from others either empowers us or inhibits us.

During my work leading conferences, many attendees have the same questions. "How do I get respect at home or work? How do I keep people from walking over me?" Essentially, what these people are asking is how to set boundaries and how to make them stick.

Boundaries are like an invisible line. I always envision myself with a bigger-than-me stick in hand, drawing a line in the sand. These lines are the limits we establish, and are how we protect ourselves from being abused, manipulated, and used by others. Our line is where the nonsense ends. Through personal boundaries, we are expressing to others that we're not a doormat or a numbskull. We are telling those around us that we have bounds that must be respected.

Building stronger boundaries doesn't alienate you from others. These boundaries allow you to express your individuality and focus on your own ideas and opinions. I'm not a fan of going along with the masses just because it appears to be the popular thing to do. We all have to develop our own ideas, thoughts, dislikes, and preferences. How else will we know when our lines have been crossed?

We live in a world with rules. Some of those rules are written, and some are unspoken, but we tend to abide by those rules. If we break those rules, we already know the consequences. As an example, when you see the sign "No Parking", that is a rule enforced by the city. They have put a boundary line in place to secure a spot for emergency personnel, or buses, or some other purpose. It's a line drawn. You understand this rule or law and you abide by it. Otherwise, what happens? You get a ticket. It'll cost you money and if you fight the ticket, it'll cost you time and probably more money.

Your personal boundaries are your rules, your law, the way you keep order in your life. Once you identify exactly what your boundaries are, you eliminate confusion from daily living. You create a space within yourself that's free of emotional clutter and mental chatter. You don't have to play a guessing game with yourself or anyone else because you know the lines drawn and compromising is out of the question.

You may have unhealthy personal boundaries without knowing it. There are many signs that point to weak borderlines including allowing others to define you, abandoning your personal rights or values in order to please others, feeling bad about saying no, taking as much as you can just for the sake of taking, letting personal relationships get too involved before you really know the other person. Before we can successfully establish boundaries with others, we must start with ourselves. It is nearly impossible to have limits with others when you don't have any with yourself.

I didn't clearly identify my personal principles until I was in my thirties. I didn't know how to put my value and belief system to work. I lacked the knowledge of applying my principles to my work and life. Had I known more about my boundaries earlier, I certainly would've made different decisions in many of my most difficult choices. Establishing a set of principles adds to our moral compass. Our principles truly do affect the way we live, how we live, and why we live. To set up your boundaries, try examining yourself and detailing what's important to you, what you value, and what you believe in. You may value happiness over influence, or you might believe loyalty is more important than success. Whatever the stance, your principles and standards affect how well you get along with others as well as how well you get along with yourself.

What another person values isn't your responsibility. It's OK if people value beauty over spirituality or creativity over security. Even if you disagree, you can respect their boundaries and avoid trying to convince them that your way is the right way. Be mindful that sometimes we discover our values through so-called mistakes or bad choices. Use those teaching experiences to help you identify what matters to you.

In this chapter, I share with you the system that I built for myself while working through my own boundary issues. Check out the Strutting Stones section at the end of the chapter for the Strut Value Chart. I believe it will help you expand your thoughts in relation to boundaries.

SAYING NO

Some days you will find yourself being emotionally unavailable to the chaos of the world, or to the problems at work, or to a friend who's back with that guy again and she's heading over to talk to you about it for the fourth time--with all of these draining encounters, you'll find yourself depleted and unable to keep it all straight. What is the worst thing that could happen if you say "no"? The people depleting your energy will find someone else to run to and overwhelm, instead of you.

There is no art or skill to it: "no" means "no". Some people have written books on why women don't or can't say "no". The easiest way to bring this word into your working vocabulary is to ask yourself, "is this something I really want to do?" "Do I really have the time for this?" "Do I even care about this issue?" People will drain you dry as long as your "yes" valve is open, and they will do it continually until you shut them off.

Working mothers have a very difficult time mastering the word "no" and sticking to this boundary because they often feel guilty about working long hours and leaving their children home alone much of the time. They won't say "no" to the kids, even when they know a mandatory "no" is needed. These same hardworking women also feel guilty about saying "no" at work because they feel like their boss might lose respect for them and they know that hard work and total dedication is needed to play the office politics game.

For an example of a boundary I hold, I have a certain number of free speaking engagements I do yearly. While there are many worthy organizations that might ask me to speak without pay, as mush as I'd like to say "yes", I can't. I have a business to run and I have to honor that. So, I already know what I'm capable of giving each year and I stand by that to cut out confusion or guilty feelings on my part.

The next time you're asked to do something, consider your own needs and the plans you have carved out. Where you place your boundaries will help you gauge which areas you need to scale back. With that pull-back comes a "no" response.

⋏ S T R U T T I N G   S T O N E S ⋏

1. What are two areas in your life that lack your authoritative voice, where do you need to speak up and do so quickly?

1.

2.

2. Step 1: Review the following table and circle the five most important items you value. (note: bottom boxes are purposely left blank for subjects that you may want to add .)

FIGURE 3: STRUT VALUE TABLE				
Honesty	Clean Language	Happiness	Success	Confidence
Open Communication	Power	Loyalty	Challenge	Excellent Heath
Spirituality	Religion	Politics	Helping	Family Time Others
Beauty	Living Purposefully	Security	Fulfillment	Food
Personal Growth	Integrity	Ethical Behavior	Money	Humility
Being Respected	Drama-Free Home	Debt-Free Living	Education	Innovation
				© Rising Media LLC 2012

Step 2: Write your top five in the space below.

My Top 5 Values Are:

1.

2.

3.

4.

5.

Step 3: Working with each one of the five qualities listed above, begin to specify boundaries that you want and need to put into place. You'll want to develop a system that brings order to your life and to the lives of those around you. If you value honesty, then you'll want to demonstrate that you're an honest person and expect that others will be honest with you. If you desire a drama-free home life, you can't be the drama queen there or at anyone else's home. Here are some questions to get things started:

- Am I living in alignment with the things I'm requesting of others?

- Why are these values so important to me?

- Have I drawn the line on these principles, and have I taught others how to respect that line drawn?

- What does it cost me when I allow others to step over my personal boundaries? How will I stop others from violating my boundaries, once they're clearly set?

- What measures am I willing to take toward someone who continuously crosses the line?

3. Decide for yourself, how will you plan to reject the requests and demands that you don't want to do or really need to do. How are you prepared to give a gracious "no" and not feel bad about your decision?

4. What are you willing to say "yes" to? Remember, knowing what you want is just as important as knowing what you don't want.

5. Over the next two months, find three things that would bring

you enjoyment. Put those items on your calendar and commit to doing them within the next two months.

1.

2.

3.

8

AUTHORITY AND HUMILITY

"Authority exercised with humility, and obedience accepted with delight are the very lines along which our spirits live." ~ C.S. Lewis

We're the dictator or the servant, self-centered or a pushover, too demanding or too soft-spoken, domineering or weak, too loud or too quiet, too strict or too relaxed, too mean or too nice, too smart or plum ignorant, a doormat or--heaven forbid--we're a bitch.

Making yourself fit into a label is one thing, but dealing with the stress that comes with it is another. You and I have bought into someone else's idea of how a woman should and shouldn't act. We've been brainwashed into believing that we have to behave one way in corporate America if we want to climb to the top, and behave another way in personal relationships if we want to be respected. We've been sold on the idea of selling other people out to make ourselves appear to be the perfect choice for the contract, the job, or the wedding ring. We've been bamboozled into believing that there aren't enough resources for everyone, so some women clutch onto the positions, not wanting to let another woman in out of fear that she'll take over.

Regardless of which side of the fence you're on, I pose this question: Why can't we just be who we are, why do we need to attach ourselves to labels and buy into old mindsets, anyway? We don't, but you don't need to fold yourself in or shrink yourself down to fit anyone's idea of who you should be. Let's think way outside the box--in fact, why not work on erasing the lines of the box and choosing to see things from a very different perspective? You can shake up a situation and combine a little bit of authority mixed in with humility or add a mixture of directness and gratitude. They might seem like opposite actions but who says you can't combine them and develop a system that gets the job done while inspiring others and leaving you empowered in the process? This is your choice; you are running your own show, so have your way with it. What's important to remember is working toward an even balance of authority and humility.

If you watch TV dramas or read the articles in magazines, most will suggest that this balancing act doesn't exist; a woman's place is usually portrayed in a different, negative light. Some business books tell a story of a grim world for women in the workplace, citing a cold and bitter climb to the top and advising that if you want to succeed in business, you've got to conform. If you buy into various brands it is a dog-eat-dog world where humility is smothered out by aggressive personalities who walk hard, talk fast, and think evil. This is untrue.

In my personal and professional experiences, I've learned

that the only way to keep peace with the external world while still honoring your internal light is to rule with honesty and directness and be respected while simultaneously respecting others. We can live and play in this space and still have an honest approach and direct communication. A lot of people go overboard teetering to one side more than the other. Your situation can all balance out with authority and humility. You can use these two attributes every day, in every situation, and walk away without any regret or remorse.

I believe the reasons these two qualities--authority and humility--aren't on societies "it list" is because they're a challenging combination to master. These two traits are foreign concepts to most people because they haven't been taught, practiced, or expected. There wasn't a prepackaged course available to instruct me how to walk that fine line between grace and power and becoming overbearing or cruel. I had to learn this balance and believe in my right to stand in it.

My progress toward this dynamic duo of humility and authority didn't happen overnight. Honing a skill is very much like working a muscle in the human body. You've got to work out and feed the muscle the right nutrients, stretch it out, and give it the rest it needs during recovery times. This is no different than incorporating these skills into your life, you've got to build up a definitive stance and try flexing it with humility. You've got to practice, you've got to be open to adapting to new thinking patterns, and you've got to be willing to stand your ground. If you are open to these challenges, you will find your own way of walking the line. You will create a tough skin laced with empathy. Don't worry about trying to find this balance; it'll come to you naturally if you provide an opening for it. Things don't just show up in our lives immediately. There has to be something in us, a yearning, or an invitation, to call them forward and allow them in. Be open to navigating your life through a lens of goodness and toughness. Embrace the opportunities that can unfold in this prideful posture, knowing full well that you can be both liked and respected—it doesn't have to be either/or.

YOU INC.

Claiming--or in some cases, reclaiming--our authority, our strut, might sound like a really big task or a daunting assignment, but it all really goes back to the basics of your self.

You are the CEO of you. You are the owner, the overseer, the magistrate, the queen, and the gatekeeper. Within the spectrum of your awesomeness is a powerful protector, a meek (or masterly) messenger, and a sanctioned specialist that no one can take from you. These traits, the benevolent gifts are yours and are already within you. It doesn't matter if you've abandoned them for ten months or ten years, your goods are still on the shelf. You are the owner and operator of the venture called you, and within the knowing of that is where you will find your authoritativeness.

You have become the expert on yourself--you're the sweet genius behind YOU, Incorporated. No one can tell you about yourself. You have been running this business 24 hours a day, 7 days a week, 365 days a year, for twenty, forty, sixty, or more years.

I really enjoy taking about the subject of empowerment with other women because I find it to be so fascinating. It amazes me how we take on the labels handed to us by others (domineering, too relaxed, doormat, or the like) and we get so lost in them that we haven't a clue how to unlearn that stigma and get back to what was there before we were tagged with these affixations.

AGGRESSION AND AUTHORITY

One of the big perceptions I had to tackle in my own journey to authority and humility was believing that aggressiveness and authority were one in the same. I believed that I wouldn't have a voice unless I was aggressive and hard, and that wasn't really who I was. Instead, I reclined back into a different label, the quiet nice girl who didn't want to bring attention to herself.

In getting my strut back and studying myself as well as many of the great leaders I admired—Jesus Christ, Dr. Maya Angelou, Gandhi, Bishop T.D. Jakes, Condoleezza Rice, Gloria Steinem, Oprah Winfrey, and many others--I noticed a beautiful lineage of passion over arrogance, determination over damming, and an unbreakable belief system.

With these people, there was aggressiveness, but it stemmed from passion and determination. Each one of the luminaries I studied is tough, but that toughness was earned. These people learned how to use toughness as fuel to keep pushing;, they developed relentlessness over a dogmatic mentality. Strutting with an authoritative posture takes confidence--confidence in knowing who you are, and a strong belief that you are deserving of whatever you're going after.

THE WHISTLING-POWERWALKING QUEEN

Being a person of authority isn't about being in the right position or having everything go your way, nor is it about having a team of people to boss around. It's about bringing aliveness, a sense of influence to the life that you are currently living. We don't wait for the next big thing to happen to start living with authority, just do it now, be it now. No matter how challenging things might be, or where you are on the promotion list, you can bring that confidence to this very moment.

During my very first job as a television news reporter with an Ohio station, I was really overwhelmed by the amount of stories I was expected to cover each day. This station was a great place to grow and learn the business, I was surrounded by some really terrific leaders that I admired. There was, as I was told: "A beast to feed" and that meant reporters and anchors had to fill every newscast with, well... news and lots of it. More often than not I was covering three different stories a day, and waiting out in the field to front my stories with live shots for the evening newscasts.

I had only been apart of the staff for a few months and one day while sitting in the newsroom, I was exhausted and I looked at the faces of my colleagues who looked equally tired and drained except one. A colleague whose workstation was next to mine hadn't really caught my eye, yet on this particular day she did.

While I was drowning in fatigue in walks Jana: this petite whistling woman with a spunky walk that exuded confidence and cheerfulness. Did I mention that she whistled? She had this thing about her, even on the toughest of the toughest days; she was the bright light in a very dim room.

So, imagine sitting at your desk worn out, sick and tired of all the running and all the bad news in the world and in walks Jana... whistling with a power walk! I must admit, I wasn't so positive, maybe even envious that she was on such a high ride while the rest of us galloped in the humdrum of the day. But one day, out of a combination or inquiry and irritation, I just had to ask, "Why are you always so happy?" She giggled and said, "My mother told me, no matter how bad things get, there are a lot more things to be happy about, so I focus on that."

Jana was no exception to the hard running of local television news reporting. She was working just as much and just as hard as the rest of us. She didn't have a superior title over any other reporters- she was, just as I was, a general assignment reporter, which meant we covered any and everything. The difference in Jana was that she was focused on other things and she chose to mindfully bring those things into the present moment.

I befriended this power-walking queen, I wanted to learn from her. The more we talked, I understood that Jana knew things wouldn't always be this way. She knew that she wouldn't always have to run so hard behind senseless news stories and that someday she would be a great contributor to the profession she genuinely loved. She also had a lot of passion for her work.

Jana's ability to focus on better days ahead brought many gifts to her present-moment living. Through thoughts of her hopes, dreams, and plans, she lived with certainty. That assured feeling boosted her authoritative stance, she brought that to her work, to her sources and to her life. She had authority with out titles and without anyone working "under" her, just her presence, her way of working and believing in something more than what the current circumstances offered was enough.

I also witnessed Jana's way of being with co-workers and how she humbled herself. From the general manager to the man cleaning the building, she held everyone in high regard while still catering to that sassy walk and a sweet whistle that would give Earle Hagen, the whistler of the Andy Griffith show, a run for his money.

AUTHORITY GONE WRONG

Your authority isn't about knowing an area of expertise or being overly smart. It's not totally about your smarts, but it has a lot to do with your demeanor, your stance, and how you relate your power to others. You might not get exactly what you want each time, but if you present yourself well, you'll feel energized by your attempts.

Your authoritative demeanor has a role in the minuscule makings of your day as well as the life-changing events. From full-time mothers to teachers, social workers, custodians, attorneys, or entrepreneurs, that dependable, trustworthy voice is there inside each one of us.

Over a decade ago, I met a woman who appeared to be very educated--she was an expert at her profession. We would occasionally bump into each other at networking events and I began noticing that, when people stopped talking about work and turned the conversations toward more trivial subjects, she locked up. This woman stopped talking and stopped sharing. It was if her light went out and she mentally left the room. One day she admitted to me that she only talked about things she knew about. Her knowledge was profound within the realm of her profession, but it stopped there.

I thought about how that must feel: imprisoning yourself in one topic, relying on one thing to talk about or share. There are so many conversations to explore, so much to learn just by listening to and asking questions of others. This lady was missing out on a chance to develop new business relationships, and possibly friendships, based on her fear of getting outside of her area of expertise. She wasn't able to really connect with others in a sincere way. Her authority was only connected to her work and nothing else.

Somehow this woman had lost her voice. She was in her fifties and surely had experienced many things in life other than her work. Because she couldn't (or wouldn't) articulate them, she lost a lot of opportunities among colleagues because she just didn't stand out in anyone's mind. She wasn't offensive, she was very professional, but in today's market, you need a lot more than "book smarts" to be remembered. This woman had a difficult time keeping a job and, while on paper she was more than capable of managing large teams, she wasn't able to really connect with groups.

Authoritativeness is in much, much more than our work. It's in our livelihood. It adds life to our ability to present new ideas to the world, and it ignites our personal goals as we strive for excellence.

NOODLE AND BONE-CRUSHING HANDSHAKES

I can't stand it--a soft, gluey handshake from an adult. It always takes me by surprise when I extend my hand for a shake and I surge right into a bowl of wet noodles. Nothing. Nothing happens in that greeting, no energy, no light--no aliveness, and nowhere to go. We can tell a lot about people by the way they stand or how they fold their arms or shift their weight, and handshakes are a great storyteller as well. I won't turn this into a chapter on body language and non-verbal communication, but I will say that our physical posture plays hand-in-hand with our ability to be influential.

A big monstrous heavy-handed handshake isn't the way to go, either. People can tell when you're overcompensating. We all need to find a happy medium that relates to how we're feeling about ourselves, what our passions are, and how engaged we are in our lives. Let's extend a handshake coming from that place. When you meet up with a personal or business contact, you will be feeling vibrant and confidant, and that should translate into your greeting.

A comfortable, strong woman stands and walks with a certain aliveness. Her head is positioned not too low or too high. Two women who exhibit great physical signs of confidence and authority are the current and former U. S. Secretaries of State, Hillary Clinton and Condoleezza Rice. We know these women are brilliant in their profession but take a closer look--each of them knows who they are, beyond the title in front of their names.

It was no surprise when, according to a newspaper article, the former Libyan ruler Moammar Gaddafi kept a photo album filled with pictures of Rice. He may not have been an exemplary man, but he knew a confident, authoritative woman when he saw one. His admiration of her was well-known.

MAKE DECISIONS QUICKLY

I missed out on a pretty good job offer in my twenties due to my inability to make a fast decision. Before I was able to get my foot in the door in television news, I was offered a position with an Ohio-based marketing firm. The position was good, but the connections and opportunity to advance would have been great. The man who ran the company was a self-made millionaire who was greatly respected throughout the global business world. I was on the brink of being mentored by this man.

He offered me the position and I told him I'd prefer to have a decision for him by the close of the following business day, which we agreed was five o'clock. He agreed that was fair. I went back and forth, hemmed and hawed over the decision facing me, undecided about the travel and the hours, but in the end I decided to move forward with the offer. After all, I'd be crazy not to take it! I was broke and chasing a career that really didn't want to be caught by me. So I called this gentleman back the following day to accept the offer, slightly before six p.m. My contact thanked me for my interest, told me the position was still open, but said he'd taken the offer off the table based on my failure to give him a decision before the 5 p.m. time I'd promised.

I was stunned. I tried making excuses, and he called me out on those too. In the days following this missed opportunity, I found fault with this man. I criticized his way of doing business, and I thought he should've given me a break. Wasn't six o'clock close enough? But the more I studied the situation and tried putting myself in his position, running a company and extending his reputation, the more I realized that I was the one who made the error.

It would take only a few weeks after that incident for me to understand the urgency in both keeping my word and making decisions promptly. The deeper I looked into it, my lackadaisical indecisiveness seemed to really be a silly cover up for procrastination. I'm sure that intelligent businessman spotted it--and who wants a procrastinator on their team?

At that time, I didn't know the security and freedom that come with knowing exactly what you want and making strong strides to go after it. Due to the sting of being rejected on that business offer, I learned if I really wanted to move forward in life, I had to kill that habit of indecisiveness and procrastination. If I really wanted to thrive, I would have to establish a different decision-making skill set. I promised to not allow procrastination to steal another opportunity from me again. That businessman taught me a tremendous lesson that is still a powerful force in my life today.

Business leader and author Napoleon Hill talked about the importance of decision-making during his lectures in the 1950's and in his many books on personal growth. We must know what we want and move toward it quickly. Successful leaders know the benefit of a sharp mind, they have made quick thinking a habit and when you know exactly what you want combined with appropriate action, many opportunities open up for you.

SAY WHAT YOU MEAN AND MEAN WHAT YOU SAY

We are clearly not living in the times of our grandmothers or even our mothers. Long gone are the slow days and easy conversations. We don't have the luxury of getting a ten-minute first impression; it's down to a mere nine seconds.

This is the case for the growing number of people who are spending a lot of time on the Internet, which nowadays are most people. According to BBC News, "the addictive nature of web browsing can leave you with an attention span of nine seconds--the same as a goldfish."

While this nine-second rule of thumb doesn't apply to everyone, it is a great reference point for the direction we're heading. We are headed toward short attention spans and poor listening skills. The good news for us Strutters is that this fact validates our reason for saying what we mean and meaning what we say.

I love being in the communication business. Meeting new people fascinates me and I enjoy hearing about their lives and dreams. I'm touched by how much you can find in common with a perfect stranger, just by sharing a conversation.

This experience can get jolted when I meet someone who is rambling on and can't make a point. They dance around the reason for speaking and lack clear direction. My loving husband has reminded me more than once that most people haven't worked in TV news, so they don't speak in sound bites. I'm cognizant of that, however, if we plan on making the right connection or getting a foot in the door, we must know how to represent ourselves. We ought to know how to convey thoughts into meaningful words.

A few years back I won a Toastmasters contest in the Table Topics category, which is an event based on extemporaneous speeches. I would strongly suggest Toastmasters experience for anyone who wants to make an influential impact in their work and life. Table Topics is a common meeting segment for Toastmasters where the speaker is assigned a subject just seconds before taking the stage. The speaker then must present a complete, though brief, speech about the topic.

When I began competing in Table Topics contests, I studied some really terrific speakers who were masters at presenting a full point in a couple of minutes. They were much better than me, and provided me with great advice on how to get better at that game.

The nine-second goldfish attention span is a tough one to accept, but we're learning all the time that we can get our point across in less time and space than ever before. Social media giant Twitter allows users 140 characters or less to make a statement, and their communication model has been embraced by millions of people all over the world.

In the important moments of your life, the times when you intend to make an impression or impact, you need to be sharp and memorable. I don't suggest that you script a response for every situation, but I would support you in developing a three-point system in your head, creating a go-to framework for any type of impromptu presentation of information. Deciding what three points you will want to hit during an introduction to a CEO or a chance meeting with a potential business partner will give you an advantage over the long-winded ramblers. Being prepared with three points for likely conversations or practicing coming up with structured comments on little or no notice will help your words flow naturally and avoid the misspeaks that will pop up during rehearsed scripts and fluster you.

I have implemented an exercise on these points in the Strutting Stones segment.

NIP IT IN THE BUD

My grandmother is a strong woman, both physically and mentally. She was always very strong and people didn't try to control her much, but there was the one woman in the neighborhood who occasionally would lock horns with my grandmother. Over the years, this woman would aim a snide remark toward my grandmother here or there.

One Sunday, Grandma took me to church with her. Her church was a small congregation with big personalities, and was located just feet from Grandma's front door. Although I was only about nine years old, once that little old preacher man started his sermon, I knew automatically how the service would end. The drummer would start tapping his drums as the preacher's breathing would deepen, the volume of his comments would increase, and then folks would start shouting and dancing (unless you've been to what some people call a "black sanctified" church, you can't really imagine this rhythmic, hysterical hoopla).

On this particular Sunday, the woman I mentioned above stood up and began her exclamations of "thank you, Jesus". She threw her hands up in the air and ran up and down the aisle, ending up back near my family's seats. This woman was hollering and the next thing I know, she threw a hand up in the air and sideswiped Grandma's head, tilting her wig. I thought, "oh, she's gonna get it!" Grandma pursed her lips together, refitted her curly wig in its spot, and kept clapping and singing praises to Jesus, nodding in agreement with the preacher. As soon as the service was over, Grandma grabbed my hand and said, "come on, baby" and she headed right toward that woman. Grandma stood closely to her so that no one else could hear what was being said as I leaned in, waiting for the tongue-lashing. "This is between you, me, and Jesus and I don't want to make any mistake about it--if you pull another one of those stunts, I'm gonna show you what praise dance is all about. Do I make myself clear?" The woman looked at me and then, wide-eyed, back at Grandma, quickly nodding in agreement.

I think Grandma had let the other small comments and offenses slide for this woman intentionally. Perhaps my grandmother didn't care much for the small stuff, but the minute the woman crossed the line, Grandma nipped her in the bud.

You and I probably won't run into someone who tries to knock us upside the head in the middle of a coming-to-Jesus moment. When we feel violated, though, we have to act on that feeling, and do so quickly. Cleaning up the drama in the midst of it takes the air out of it. Otherwise, hurt feelings and resentment can build, and days later that negativity will be bleeding over into another household or department at work. Move quickly to resolve conflict.

WOMAN TO WOMAN

There are women out there who don't want to share their resources with you. They don't want to teach or lead younger women in the right direction. Perhaps they don't lend a helping hand because of their own insecurities or jealousies, or due to a fixed way of believing and behaving. These women might not even know why they feel the way they do. They may not realize that there is enough positivity in life for everyone. Hoarding power or position doesn't elevate anyone or promote their advancement; instead, it slowly catches up with them in unsuspecting ways. This is just more evidence in how the law of karma works. Trust me, these malicious people get theirs, too.

A lot of people still believe in that old saying "good guys finish last"...and that's according to whom? I tend to follow a very different beat and that is the one that says "cream always rises to the top".

People who connive, manipulate, and browbeat their way to the top might appear to have it made, but they soon reap what they sow. It is a universal law: what you do unto others is done unto you. This applies to both the good gals and the not so good gals.

The law of attraction, Karma and other names tell us that what we put out into the world is guaranteed to come back to us. The Law of Retribution where "every wrong action or crime brings it's own punishment" explains it another way. We have Biblical principles to back up these theories as well as scientist through Newton's Third Law of Motion which states: that every action has an equal and opposite reaction. Spiritual teacher Swami Sivananda shares his philosophy of energy attraction in another way, "He who hurts another man, hurts himself first. He who cheats another cheats himself first." All of the spiritual advisors and teachers are essentially saying the same thing: how we treat others is how we treat ourselves and what we do to others is already done unto us.

When I was considering making another try at television news after initially leaving the field, I interviewed with a female manager who was very unfriendly to me from the start, for no reason that I could discern. On that same day, I met with quite a few people who were all very kind and informative, and it seemed like they were interested in me, as well. The woman who was in charge of the hiring process, however, was not warm or friendly toward me at all. I thought that perhaps she was having a rough day, but when she walked me to the rear of the newsroom, curtly thanked me for my time, and showed me the stairwell out rather than the elevator I had taken up, I knew then that this was someone who just was not interested in reaching out and building up a fellow human being. I later learned after speaking with a few employees and members of the community, that this manager did not hold her fellow sisters in high regard. From that information, I was able to draw a possible conclusion on how this woman felt about herself. If she truly had a problem honoring other women in her environment, she had a problem honoring herself. I understood that this woman's attitude was negative to me because she was unhappy with herself. She gave every sign of taking out her frustration on other women, especially those who strive to be positive and upbeat in life, as I was. I thought that this type of behavior was a thing of the past, I thought the "mean girl" mentality was left back in junior high school, or I was at least hoping that was the case as I tried to give this female manager a pass on her foul behavior.

I have a very dear friend who is retired from the educational system. During a phone chat around the time of her sixty-fifth birthday, I expressed my frustrated feelings that some other women were trying to trip me up in a certain situation I was handling. I told her that I thought the cattiness and drama stopped in high school. To my surprise, she said to me, "Raquel, you will go through it your entire life," she said. "I'm still experiencing it and it isn't even slowing down." My friend is in her seventies now and she still has run-ins with women who don't want to elevate each other or who actively are trying to tear down other women.

I'm not suggesting that women give other women a free ride simply because they're women but what I am saying is that women don't need to be harsh toward one another, either. Even if I'm not a good fit for the job, don't mistreat me just because. This "there isn't enough room for both us" mentality is a sickness breathing through our sisterhood and it prevents some women from extraordinary opportunities.

Some research in an article "Having a Woman Boss Doesn't Help Women Get Ahead", shows that having women in high positions usually doesn't improve the number of women hired nor the amount of money female workers earn. I can't help but wonder what Susan B. Anthony, Harriet Tubman, Gloria Steinem and the other trailblazing women would feel about their hard fight for equality and our promise to collaborate with and help another.

So we can't eliminate the mindset some women have as it relates to mentoring or honoring each other, nor can we fix them; we just need to stay on top of our game and make certain that, as much as some women hate on other women, we are loving on one another. It is so very empowering to focus more of your energy on assisting a sister, rather than worrying about why someone just passed you over or snubbed you when you needed their help to improve yourself. You and I have got to come from a different perspective, we need to make sure that for every one hater there are one hundred strutters! There are enough other sources of friction in our lives that we should strive to make our woman-to-woman transactions and interactions run smoothly and benefit both parties.

HUMILITY

Humility is reverent concern and, while it is a state of mind, most of it begins and ends in the soul. It is through compassion that we're able to humble ourselves to see others as God sees them. There is no division in humility, just a subtle devotion that is tender and loving beyond measure. There are no boundaries to humility; it's free flowing, everlasting, and available to you in an instant.

There are layers of gifts in humility, which somehow go to a deeper level than the heart. Humility spills over into unsuspecting areas in our lives. While we don't display humility with hopes of receiving blessings from the good deed, a person who purposely moves herself out of the spotlight with the intention of honoring and serving other people almost always reaps beautiful unforeseen rewards.

My mother basically forced me into beauty pageants when I was a teenager as a way of winning scholarship money for college. I wasn't a big fan of pageantry because of the meticulous preparations and nervous energy but I met so many fantastic people, some who made many lasting impressions on my life.

In the 1990's I won the title of Miss Ohio World. Midway through my reigning year, I found myself surrounded by some really beautiful young women at the Miss World America pageant in Mexico. It was a unique experience that included a very tiring week of media promos and rehearsals leading up to the televised event.

A few nights before the actual event, all the girls were on stage rehearsing and I didn't feel a win coming my way. Pageants are such a mind game, sometimes you just want to stop thinking about how you'll smile or which way you'll turn around and wave. So while the rehearsal was happening, I sat off to the side of the stage with a few other girls. A man, "Jim", had been working on the set most of the day was adjusting a few things on the stage near us, and he started talking to us. It didn't seem like he was having a good day, so he just started talking about the show and how we were feeling. He seemed to be filling dead air with small talk.

Our minds were pretty occupied with other things such as

winning or losing, trying to remember all the chorography, and figuring out what type of questions the judges would ask, so no one really responded to Jim. I looked him over and he looked a bit rumpled and tired. I felt something for him, not sympathy or sadness, but something told me to stop thinking about winning or losing and just talk to him. I began talking to him and asking questions about his trade and later about his family. The following days I would find myself ending up right back on that side of the stage when my group was not rehearsing, and Jim and I would say hello and share some small talk.

At the end of the week, it was show time. After a parade of routines and cheerful introductions, I sat on the sidelines, watching the top ten--which did not include me--dwindle down to a final winner. Just like that, the big world contest was over and I had not prevailed. Disappointed, I was leaving backstage to find my family and that Jim stopped me in the hallway, still dressed in worn blue jeans and a soiled white T-Shirt. He asked if I would be open to an opportunity to model for a New Jersey-based company, as well on the auto-show circuit in Detroit. I told him yes to both, but I was unsure of how Jim could make anything happen since he was in the construction business, not model management. I gave him my information and forgot about his offer as I busied myself getting ready to go home.

A few short weeks after that pageant, I received two phone calls. Both of the calls led to work that Jim mentioned--not only were the offers legitimate, but they were beneficial to me in my career at the time. Through these opportunities, I landed a year-long modeling contract with an auto service company and an audition that led to a spokesmodel position in another industry.

As it turns out, Jim wasn't just a contractor--he owned the company that had built the set for the competition that week. I found out later that he was impressed with me taking the time to talk and share with him when he was pushing through a tough week. "He thought the world of you, when you asked about his kids and wife and if they had a dog," Jim's contact at the New Jersey business told me. Apparently, Jim was a real genuine person who enjoyed people and in that atmosphere, surrounded by beauty pageant contestants, he didn't find a lot of genuine camaraderie.

During the pageant, when I asked about his work, Jim never told me he owned the company. Maybe that was part of his plan to see if I had the personality he was seeking, but the information about his true position would not have mattered to me anyway. My very first job was as a janitor, spending an entire summer cleaning a school building. While I didn't like the job, I learned to respect the hard work and anyone working "behind the scenes". I never saw Jim or spoke with him again, but my time with him and the resulting benefit to my career reconfirmed the beauty of humility. That experience led to two fantastic job positions for me. While I wasn't expecting anything from Jim other than a few minutes of pleasant conversation, it was so rewarding to get the professional boost. It was assuring to know that those blessings came of me taking the focus off myself and just giving of my time and attention to someone else. Regardless of whether it's time or conversation, greatness can come out of the action of simple giving to others.

No matter our position, rank, class, or race, we're all the same, even if we're sitting in a beaded evening gown talking to man who's nailing a stage together. We don't rely on blessings forming out of humility. We don't hold any expectations when we are truly humble, but when you're in that space, you never know who is holding your next blessing.

You can be authoritative and be unassuming at the same time.

You can be inspired while assisting others to discover their own inspiration. You don't always have to run the show, but when you do, you can run it while serving others.

Humbling ourselves to recognize the sameness and oneness charging through our fellow sister or brother guides us to a state of grace. Humility gives us permission to see the good in ourselves and in others, no matter how bleak things may seem on the outside. Humility is a simplistic reminder that we're more alike than we are different.

⚑ STRUTTING STONES ⚑

1. What limiting labels do you need to eliminate and what empowering positions can you now embrace? For example:

~~Weak~~ ⟶ Competent   ~~Passive~~ ⟶ Passionate   ~~Aggressive~~ ⟶ Direct

2. What two things can you commit to doing to enhance your authoritative skills using the principles discussed in this chapter?

   1.

   2.

3. Review the "Say What You Mean and Mean What You Say section on Three Talking Points. What are the three points that are important for others to know about you? It doesn't matter if you are meeting a new love interest or interviewing for a job, what are three points you want to convey about yourself and your values?

1.

2.

3.

4. Search your mind for a time when you were sincerely humbled
by the kindness or thoughtfulness of someone else. How did their
generosity make you feel? How would it make you feel to be able
to share a similar experience with others?

Commit to acting kindly or thoughtfully at the next opportunity--
and the one after that, and the one after that--particularly
if you are tired, distracted, or otherwise disinclined to be kind or
thoughtful at first.

9

ANSWERING THE
3 A.M. LOVE CALL

"Desire awakens only those things that are thought possible." ~ *Rene Descartes*

How many times have you heard the phrase, "let things come to you," and you had no idea what that meant or how to go about making it happen? I used to think it was some old tale created by a group of wrinkly-faced churchwomen wearing big feathery hats. They were my great-grandmother's friends, and they seemed to have had secret meetings with God and through their experiences, they got a direct message from Him. Now that I'm slowly becoming one of these old ladies, I'm getting the idea that's sort of what it's all about: letting things come into my life through a higher power, a higher form of intelligence.

Letting things come to you is what the teachers of our time mean when they encourage you to be still and know that the answers are within. We have instant access to our dreams and desires through prayer, meditation and contemplation, and what's so fascinating to me is how each one of us has something different brewing within us. How is it that there are ideas planted in you that no one else has ever thought of? You have dreamed up business deals, ways of strengthening your family, and innovative ways to maneuver tough times without much help from the outside world. All of that began with a thought that came from within. Maybe it didn't wake you up at 3 a.m. but it was born in you.

Three a.m. is used as a metaphor here. Whatever you're seeking might come in the middle of the night, during an afternoon walk, or through a chance encounter with another person; how the inspiration gets to you doesn't matter. What's important is that you are listening and you're able to feel the love and guidance from something greater than you. It's important that you are able to connect with that power and see that you're here, on this earth, for a reason--that you're cared for, and your ability and talents are needed in this world in this very moment.

OUT OF THE BLUE MESSENGERS

About two months into my contract as a reporter with a TV station in Dallas, I was excited to be in a vibrant city and I was enjoying learning about the bigness of Texas living. At that time of transformation in my life, I happened to read a newspaper story about a woman pastor who had a ministry in North Dallas. The AIDS resource center she was heading up in Africa caught my attention. I wanted to meet this woman and share her vision with our audience, so I set an interview up with her for a Saturday morning.

The morning of the interview was the first heavy rain of the wet season in Dallas. The weather was gloomy but our tasks for the day were still on schedule. As my cameraman and I arrived at her large church, the pastor greeted us with very warm eyes and a soft voice. I immediately felt comforted and welcome in her presence, I was drawn to her. My cameraman Jay, and I set up for the interview in her tiny but cozy office on the second floor of the church building. While the room was already small, the pastor asked if there was a way I could sit closer to her during our interview. I had no idea why, but Jay arranged our chairs to be nearer to each other before we started taping.

The interview went well, and I thanked the pastor for her time. As we were preparing to leave, she asked if I would mind if she had a word with me alone. I asked Jay to excuse us, saying that I'd be right out so we could head to our next story. The pastor and I sat down and she grabbed my hands. "Sweetheart," she said, "I don't know what you're doing, but this ain't it. This is not where your calling is. I see something much bigger for you."

I tensed up and tried to fight back the tears, as she wasn't aware that, just a few months earlier, I had packed up everything I owned and took a chance leaving Ohio for Dallas without knowing a single person in Texas. This woman had no way of knowing how big of a gamble I had taken on the job, or the sacrifices I had made in my personal life to get there. She did not know my personal back-story or my concerns and weaknesses. She didn't know the aches I felt from the commuter marriage my husband and I agreed on until he could relocate his work. This woman didn't know me at all, but somehow she could see into the deepest part of me.

She went on, "I'm not saying you're not good at it. I thought you interviewed me very well, but I just feel God's pull on you and you've got to be ready to move on." The tears rolled down my face and she cried too. "I'm not trying to recruit you to my ministry, and we'll probably never see each other again but I had to say what was put in my heart."

Indeed, I never saw her again.

A few years after I'd moved on from that position--which she's right, was not the path for me--I tried to find her through old news scripts and her church, which I learned no longer exists. I even contacted my former cameraman and asked him to help locate her, to no avail. I wanted to reconnect with this insightful woman and thank her for sharing such a necessary message with me, but it seems like she only existed for that small window of time when I needed her.

People can come by our way for just a brief dash of time and a message can flow right through them to us. I've never had a big bright vision and an actual voice of God telling me what to do and where to go, but I have had pieces of light and inspiration. These small nudges have come to me on rainy days and sunny days, they've happened inside a church, at a bank drive-through, and in line at the grocery store. I've received messages from wrong-number phone calls and in the pages of a book that just happens to fall open on page 118, revealing the exact answer I needed. These love calls come in many forms and are always accompanied by the very thing that you need at that moment in your life.

Hearing that concerned message delivered with love by that pastor was just what I needed at that time. I'd been feeling very detached from myself and the Source--what I call my higher power. I felt lost, and I was trying my best to cover it up. When she told me of her concern for me, I knew she was right but I didn't know anything else. I don't recall ever crying with a stranger the way I did that day, but there was something so very comfortable and familiar about her.

Sometimes it's difficult to discern these messengers, we don't know if they are truly sent by God or if they have a different agenda. I knew this woman's message was genuine for a few reasons and the most important of those reasons was I didn't feel a bit of fear. Considering that I had just relocated my life to Texas, hearing her words wasn't the greatest news but her message didn't permeate sadness or fear. Her news somehow helped me breathe a bit lighter. When such moments happen in your life, do a body-check- that is, feel the sensations that are happening as you receive the news. We're living in a time where some people run cons preying on predicting the answers to all of our problems or prophesying for a profit. Be very leery of people who claim they will deliver you from your problems if you help them and also keep a watchful eye for those who outright tell you that they're a "healer", "prophet" or anything else related to God's work. In no way am I suggesting that such people don't exist but I am saying that their actions will speak over their vocal chords. When God blesses someone's ability to spiritually connect with others, we see and feel their work, we don't hear them talking it up.

Another reason I believe the pastor's words were from the Divine Source was because I didn't have a private agenda- that is, I wasn't expecting nor seeking anything from this woman. I wasn't fixed on seeing things a certain way. It all happened out of the blue. There was a feeling of "rightness" in my mind, heart and gut, it all felt right.

Enlightened messages can surely be revealed to you in others ways as well. There was a time where a strong message of truth was revealed to me by my own, willful initiation. I was seeking to connect with someone who could help me get my business started in the Ohio area, I didn't know who but I knew that I needed some help, some advice or introductions to influential people. I made a few phone calls and was told to give a woman named Roxanne Kaufman Elliott a call, I was told that she could connect me to the right people.

I picked up the phone to call this woman, thinking at least she could hand me off to the right people. She not only answered my call, she suggested we meet. We did and within this petite, red-head was a powerhouse negotiator, businesswoman and respected community leader. We clicked instantly and I knew this was a woman I wanted to be around, a woman I could learn some things from, but I wasn't expecting such a spiritual-sister connection to her. I knew the name Roxanne rocked, but I had no idea how this woman would embrace me and become such a powerful force in my life.

Her messages were strong, there were so many and they continue to come. Although I made the call to her, thinking she was just another contact to more contacts, I had no idea that we would share in this work and in a friendship that not only uplifts me but also greatly serves my life.

OBEDIENCE

Since I was a child, I always felt like there was something special for me to do. I didn't feel more special than other kids, I just knew that there was something in me that had to be released. I didn't know what it was, which made it all the more difficult to try to explain it to others and convince myself to believe in something that was just that: something I couldn't articulate.

So, after the pastor confirmed my deepest suspicion, I began asking questions. I asked God to reveal to me where I needed to be and tell me what I needed to know, and then I began to listen. My first several answers came to me through various channels but, because I didn't like the direction these love calls were sending me, I ignored them. Maybe that wasn't really a message, I thought, maybe it was busy chatter in my mind or maybe just that heavy cream sauce on the linguine I had for dinner! I got tangled up in my own fallibility. The answers were certainly coming, but I wasn't obedient to my own request; I wasn't listening. I felt so foolish when I realized what I was doing. I was so obsessed with what the world around me was telling my head that I neglected what was being communicated to me through my spirit.

It took some time before I learned how to totally let go and relinquish my need to be in control. I had to learn to trust the process, not sometimes, but all the time. I worked hard at obeying the love calls that were being sent to me, and the more I tuned in to that spiritual channel, the more information I received.

I've talked with and interviewed many people, and I've noticed a recurring theme in powerful women: they know when to listen to a love call. They know about the prize that can be inside just one idea. They understand that they could be just one decision away from tremendous rewards and successes. They know that those small inspirations can be life-changing.

Our ideas and creativity don't come from outside of us; they all begin on the inside. Inspiration is born within us and that's also where it's nurtured. Our heart, our self, is where we design and build-- we're our own workshop. To move to a new level, to regain your strut, develop what's inside you first. Then, when you know who you really are, take that newfound power and certainty to the reports, proposals, relationships, and other areas of your life, outside yourself.

If you do this process the other way around, those outside items are just something on your to-do list. Without internal intention, your external tasks are not special or inspired, and probably won't reap the results you're hoping for. Bring the brilliance to your life--accept the gift from that love call, the specialness that only you can bring. Take what's been given to you and build on it. Once you've given yourself all that you can to the best of your ability, you can rest in that completion without second-guessing or worrying, because you've given your absolute best.

To help become obedient to this call and open to those messages, start keeping a notebook and pen next to your bed for those unexpected but much appreciated 3 a.m. love calls. There have been times when I had to scribble out a short phrase in the dark and then go back to sleep. Other times, there was so much of this sweet cake of inspiration to eat, I'd go to another room and write a page or two, or three, or however much was willing to come out. I'd keep writing until the flow stopped. Listen to what's being said and honor it by paying attention.

LITTLE VOICES

"Pick up that piece of litter." "Say hello to her." "Turn around to make sure that man isn't following you." "Save a backup to that document." All of these wise words stem from this little voice inside your head, your intuition. You and I can probably agree that the inside of our head is a busy place, with voices constantly talking to us and telling us what to do and what not to do. It can be a bit chaotic at times, so knowing where all this advice is coming from will help you in deciding which advice to take.

A human brain has over seventy thousand thoughts per day. It's a safe assumption that most of those thoughts are random and automatic thoughts that you are not controlling, that aren't related to intuition, and that aren't thoughts that you are consciously choosing to have. For example, when you're driving to work and you get to the parking lot without remembering passing any red lights or seeing any traffic, you were in auto-pilot thinking about a zillion things that removed you from the present activity.

When the mental chatter of your mind is on overload, take a time-out and try to make a distinction of where those thoughts are coming from. Closely examine the thoughts that are calling for action. Review them so you have a stronger foundation to launch from. Ask yourself, is this thought motivated by ego--the part of you that seeks to please, seeks attention, seeks to outdo, and works to make others right or wrong? Or is this thought supported by my true self--the part of you that doesn't seek recognition but urges you to do the right thing?

Let's use the "pick up that piece of litter" instructive voice as an example. What's behind that thought? Are you picking up a scrap of paper to show others that you're a clean, dignified resident who cares about the earth, or are you picking it up because you actually do care about the earth? Would you pick it up if no one else were watching?

This has been my guide for following those little voices that talk to me throughout my life. With practice exploring the motivations behind these voices, you can get really quick at deciphering what is really influencing your thoughts and urges. The more you honor your true voice, the more you'll strengthen it. The more you honor the ego and false urges, the more you will strengthen them. The choice is yours.

WRITE NEW RULES AND EXCEED THEM

Once you decide to partner with that "love call" drawing you to your true self, a lot happens. A lot of old ideas and beliefs will shift in your life when you open yourself up to new ideas. You will create a larger space for creativity to flow. You'll want to develop a strong system to back up all of these inspiring new ideas; you may desire to have a new surface to work on and a new playground to explore.

Your willingness to write new rules solidifies that you are in a trusting place in regards to the love call. By giving yourself the freedom to change, you send a strong signal to your brain that you are betting on great things happening so much that you're already in the planning stages for those changes.

Diana Nyad knows about writing new rules and exceeding them. In 1975, she swam around Manhattan Island in seven hours and 57 minutes. In 1979 she swam 102.5 miles from North Bimini Island, Bahamas Juno Beach Florida (without a shark cage), setting a new world record. She was a young, vibrant, strong woman when she broke records, but she never lost her love for her passion.

Now in her sixties, Nyad plows forward, charting new territory and redefining age as it relates to stamina, well-being, and personal commitment. She continues to plan for improving herself. "I think that sixty is when many people hit their prime," she said in a magazine interview. "We elect many of our presidents in their sixties," she relates, "at that age, people are full of ideas and their best self. I wanted to dig into my potential and bring out my best self."

In 2011, she was on the brink of becoming the first person to swim between Cuba and Florida without a shark cage. After nearly thirty hours of fighting heavy currents and problems with asthma, though, Nyad reluctantly ended her swim, only to almost immediately start planning to try again in 2012.

This prominent long distance swimmer has told reporters many times over that her efforts toward these amazing feats aren't about trying to prove anything to anyone, but are instead about personal determination and how she chooses to live life.

Nyad has clearly given a new meaning to old sets of rules about age and tough goals. She has declared that our sixties is a time for living bigger, stronger lives. She is not only changing the rules but also living by them.

You might not be a world record long-distance swimmer, but what areas in your life needs a new set of rules? Look for opportunities to set rules that force you outside of the norm. Pursue goals that-- when achieved--will bring a whole new meaning to your life.

PRAYER & FAITH

Before I pray, I observe where I'm coming from. I do a self-check in relation to energy. Am I coming from a depleted space of sorrow and sadness, or am I coming from a place of total faith supported by gratitude? The reason this is so important to recognize is because the energy we give out into the world is what we get back. This law of cause and effect is also true in relation to prayer. When you take your problems and praises to God, be mindful that He already knows what's in your heart and mind. He wants to know that you have faith that He's going to take care of you as you continue applying yourself toward your goals and desires.

I never thought I would quote rapper 50 Cent in this book, but his take on faith and prayer was spot on. "You should either pray or worry, don't do both," he told Oprah Winfrey during an interview. "If you pray and then worry, how do you think that makes God feel?"

Worry is the opposite of faith, so if you are praying or meditating on a situation that has caused anguish or worry, that moment of connecting with your God is not the place to display those negative emotions. Focusing on anger and worry only brings more of it back to you.

Because we are human, we worry when we can't pay our bills, when the marriage is breaking up, or when the kids are acting out, but God wants to see us rise above that human condition. He wants to see where our true faith lies.

I truly believe one of the reasons why it took me so long to recover from many of my setbacks in the past was because I grieved so hard. I was simmering in grief, pain, and disappointment. When I prayed, I came from those disempowering places. Now, looking back, I can see why I kept getting more of that same kind of negativity back--it was because I was putting so much of it out.

One day, I changed my conversation with God. I corrected my approach. I started with one line: "thank you, God, for putting breath in my body." Some days that's all I could say. After some time, I moved up to "please show me the way." I had to put a stop to the pity-party praying and put all of my faith in the only power that was capable of moving me out of that very dark time. I had to develop a way of praying that would deliver me from past pains, prayers that would guide me every so closely to the purpose of my life. I developed the mantra: Lead with faith or leave it alone. And that one line has brought a significant amount of order to my life.

⋏ STRUTTING STONES ⋏

1. Clear a space off of your nightstand and keep a notebook and pen handy. Create a folder on your computer or in your file drawer and title it whatever you wish to call it (yes, I use "love calls", but use what works for you) and drop in any articles or notes that pop at you. You don't need to know why you're drawn to these inputs, just file it. In your cell phone, open a blank note and use it to type in ideas or other information that you encounter when you're away from your real or virtual folder. Invent a new system to record and keep these inspirations; avoid being caught without a way to track your creative call.

2. Recall a time when you may have ignored a "love call" that showed up again later via someone else independently suggesting that you should follow the same path, or you see your idea sprout up on TV or a bookshelf. How did you feel seeing this confirmation of a missed inspiration after you know you received, and ignored, a message about it earlier?

3. List three times when a message came for you and you just knew it was right. How did you feel, what was it about this message or the incident that told you that it was right for you?

    1.

2.

3.

4. During quiet time, prayer, or meditation, think about one thing
you can feel grateful for. If you're experiencing a challenging
time, coming from a place of gratitude, rather than anger, can put
you in a different frame of mind, which gives off a different
energy.

5. Diana Nyad is just one woman who is making new rules, she's
setting new goals and plowing forward. What are five new rules
you need to add to your life that ups the ante? Go bigger than
you ever have before. Make sure that they are realistic and
inspire you to stretch yourself to become the person that you
desire to be. Don't make these rules doable today or next week—
make them big enough that you've got to strengthen your mind
and maybe your body to get there. Make a change happen within
you in order to put you in that place of personal commitment.

1.

2.

3.

4.

5.

PERFECTLY POSITIONED

"Consider it pure joy, my brothers, whenever you face trials of many kinds, because you know that the testing of your faith develops perseverance. Perseverance must finish its work so that you may be mature and complete, not lacking in anything."
James 1:2-4 (NIV)

What would be your advice to someone who has gone through a lot of challenges, a lot of ups and downs, twists and turns, jumping through hoops, bumping into doors, and being kicked in the teeth? Would you tell her to give up or keep fighting? Would you tell her to go hide or come out fighting? Since you have come through a journey with me in these pages, my spirit tells me that you would encourage her to keep moving. I'd want to see the underdog become the comeback kid. I'd cheer for her and bet on her because she's faced so much and she keeps getting back up. I'd say she was a winner because those who go through hard times are being primed for something bigger. They're being prepared for something big, extraordinary even--they may not be able to even fathom what's behind the trials. Are you that fighter, that kid who has it in you to be great?

I have a very kind friend, "Lori" who has been in the same line of work for thirty years. She is a stunning woman who doesn't pride herself on her beauty but on her inner strength and character. People around her recognize her appealing appearance as well as an overflow of grace and integrity on the inside. She has a pleasurable disposition and people always want to be around her.

Lori is very smart and extremely articulate, but she doesn't speak up for herself very much. When dealing with complicated colleagues or mean managers, she bites her tongue, to keep peace in the workplace. This silencing hasn't always helped her. Over the years, her reluctance to speak up has caused much corrosion in her self-esteem and overall well-being, but she continues to smile and be elegantly graceful. She has been passed over for raises repeatedly, while colleagues and newcomers make more money than her greater experience.

Over the many years of our friendship, I have repeatedly suggested that Lori consider moving out of that career and finding something else that would support her need to be in service. I wanted to see her achieve the respect I thought she deserved. She resisted, citing her commitment to the people who benefit from her work. She was dedicated to her purpose, even though she was submerging her true self to do it.

YOU'RE READY WHEN YOU'RE READY

Before I decided to write this book, Lori hit some really low moments. She was being severely mistreated and harassed by others. Because I had lived through my own days of being a doormat, refusing to speak up for myself, I wanted to rescue her somehow. I thought the years she had put up with all of the hypocritical office policies and politics and shenanigans of disgruntled colleagues was way too much time. One day, something happened.

Lori suddenly found her own strength and I could hear it through a deepening tone in her voice, and her thoughts translated into short and succinct expressions, she wasn't dancing around anything anymore. I was so overjoyed to share in this transformation, I said to myself, "finally, she's had enough."

I must admit, I was wondering what took her so long. At her request, I had been sharing my strategies--the same strategies you have just read—and she was sharing some of her own empowerment research with me, but she still wasn't moving. I then had to remember my own rough rides and the time that it took me to get my head right about what I needed and wanted to do. My time isn't your time, and Lori's time isn't my time, either. We are all being tested on various levels. We're given time to hone perseverance. We must develop ourselves and go through changes, and even sometimes experience mistreatment from others. We're all clothed with completion at different times, under different circumstances.

It wasn't a week after Lori first displayed that firmness in her voice that her circumstances changed. One of the main culprits in her office was removed from the situation, and other trouble-causing coworkers moved to other departments or different shifts. I must believe that the situation changed because Lori changed. She had finally found her voice, as well as her authentic power. She assured me that she didn't complain or wish ill on others, but I feel strongly that her personal power resulted in the immense improvement in her personal situation. I think Lori grew into herself when she was ready, and the energy and sheer power of her magnificence moved obstacles out of the way. When that negative energy was removed from her work environment, it made space for blessings in her life. The next week, she got a raise, a pretty big one. Her empowerment and resulting success all happened in her own time.

REPACKAGE IT

You discover your passion and purpose, not necessarily through success, but through pain and perseverance. We don't go through hard times for nothing. There is a reason for adversity and a process that must be endured before improvement arrives. Take what you know, take what's been done to you--the good and the bad--and repurpose it for a greater use. Repackage your difficulties and see them for what they really are: testaments to your towering strength, and a throwback to the essentiality of your spirit.

When I asked Lori about what clicked in her when she came into herself, she told me that she had been thinking about all of the things that had happened to her in her life. She said these thoughts opened her eyes to the fact that, even though she was a good-hearted person, good things weren't happening to her, and she knew she needed to make some changes. I respect this woman and I know that she is extremely smart, but what I really wanted to know was what made this time different from her many approaches to her frustrations in the past. She told me that, in the past she was busy trying to fix the small stuff, when she needed to focus on the one big thing staring her right in the face: "the inability to ask for what I want."

PROMOTE YOURSELF

Lori prided herself on being of high morale and the people who know her well would certainly agree on her many fine qualities. Lori's mother raised her on good principles and her mother taught her to work hard. Lori followed that advice to the "T" but still didn't understand why she kept coming up short.

You may recognize yourself in this pattern, you're a good person, you treat others fairly but they don't often return that treatment to you. You might be a hard worker, doing more work than your manager's boss, taking work home and allowing it to spill over into your weekends but you keep hoping and praying that someone will notice your drive and determination. Most of us might not know to speak up and ask for what we want or bring our effort to the attention of our superiors. When Lori changed her demeanor and began handling her problems differently, things began to change. Never sit around and assume the higher-ups are aware of your contributions, inconsistencies in pay and desires to move forward, you've got to make them aware of it through direct contact and a willingness to promote yourself to greatness.

GIVE IT AWAY

This life is about more than just you and your story. It's about what you do with your resources and who you impact during this journey. Success isn't about the fame or fortune, or the number of people reporting to you in the office or following you on social media. True inspiration, strutting your stuff, is about what you're giving, why you're giving it, and how it translates into love for yourself and for others.

Take your afflictions and make them your aids. Squeeze the best possibility out of every lemon that's handed to you. Be grateful to your past, which has been a powerful teacher to you. Everything that happened to you, as well as the way you deal with it and build on it, adds up to the totality of who you are. It's all a recipe for the making of you. Use your past and what you've worked through to identify with others so that you can be of service to them.

You wouldn't be able to understand what it's like to eat scraps from the neighbors unless you've done it. You wouldn't know the responsibility placed on the eldest of five unless you were that oldest child. You wouldn't identify with being on welfare after loosing your job and still trying to feed your children unless it happened to you. You couldn't understand what it feels like to be raised in foster care unless you were.

You know what it's like to endure whatever you had to go through. We often turn this litany of past wrongs done to us into a sad, sappy story of "woe is I." We dance at a pity party, forgetting that we have a choice to use those negative experiences as power fuel to rev up our sense of place in this world. We should know and fully embrace the notion that we have the power to turn those hardships into gems of wisdom.

As much as you have survived, you should feel strong, so empowered that you kick open the door with a roar, stating your existence--you made it! You're alive! Now take that, and give it to two, or three, or more other women who need examples of survivors. Give to women who need a real, live story to relate to and connect with. Give them the type of truth you needed or wanted when things were bleak.

I have a space on my website titled "Stellar Sisters" where we post pictures and stories of women who are not only strutting in life, but are reaching back and giving to other women. I want to celebrate the she-ro in us all. You can mentor another woman through your powerful story and help her see that we all experience rough waters, but it's how you ride that wave that counts. I want to celebrate you for getting to that place in your life. So please, give another woman a hand, and we'll all applaud you.

STAY IN YOUR OWN LANE

Many of my colleagues seemed to have advanced faster than me. It appeared that they had more influence and more trappings of success than I did, even though we were roughly the same age. While I was checking out SallySue and BestyAnn, my own path to success was faltering. As soon as you start concentrating on beating or outdoing the other gals, you'll forget what's important. Do what you know how to do, do the best you can, and let the rest take care of itself.

It takes energy to mind your colleagues or neighbors business. It takes effort to meddle in the workings of their world. When you're in a race to build a stronger life, a better business or stronger relationships, by the time you look over to see what others are doing, you've exerted energy needed for your own moves.

I ran track in high school and had a pretty awesome coach who taught me how to mind my own business in getting to the finish line. One thing that he said which I have applied to my life is this "By the time you turn to see where you're opponent is, you've wasted precious seconds for the race- just run and don't worry where everyone else is."

DON'T TAKE MORE THAN YOU NEED

It's a sad but true fact that some women will spend their entire lives hiding. They may not ever break down the wall of pretense and discover their real firepower. Those are the same women who usually fail to help other women out. They have a mentality that "there's not enough for both you and me".

There is an abundance of resources readily available for you, me, and the millions of women across the world. There is enough food, water, shelter, money, pretty shoes, and love for all of us. Don't fall for scarcity because God created an overflow of everything you and I need or want.

As you readjust your life and step up to the positioning plate, you'll find plenty of goods. Take what you need, but don't take it all just because you can or just because it's available to you. Leave something for, or pass it on to, others.

Satisfy yourself with the fruits of your labor, but deny the urge to always want more and always think you need more. This is greed speaking, and once it makes its appearance, a decaying of the spirit usually follows.

We're living in a world where greed is smeared through corporate America, politics, our education system, and even in our churches. People have dismissed the needs of others and fragrantly ignored the call to make sure that everyone has enough.

We all come from the same source, the Omega, Jehovah, the God of your understanding. Even through religious differences or political opinions, we're all one, we are all extensions of God. Therefore, we have a duty to make sure that we take care of ourselves and have enough grace to consider our fellow sisters and brothers.

Whether you live in a mansion or a one-room apartment, if there is something left over from a blessing, take what you need from any resource, tangible or intangible, and find a way to pass on the rest to others.

Greed is counterproductive for the woman who has her strut in high gear. It stifles her and changes the trajectory of her life. As your cup fills up and runs over, appreciate that blessing. Lay down in it, and rejoice in the fact that you have what you need and want. Be delighted in your ability to provide for yourself, and celebrate the successes that God has given you and continues to give. You are a woman of influence. Build on that and extend yourself through your home, community, and your country with the intention that those ripples will be felt around the world.

GET ON THE TRAIN

As I was sharing my reason for writing this book to a dear friend, I explained how I hope the principles within these pages might help guide others to live a more purposeful, powerful life. My friend expressed a beautiful interpretation involving a train ride to "somewhere" and the similarities it shares with life's twists and turns. I pondered the idea and found some distinctions to this train metaphor.

Life is like a train ride. In the beginning, we're waiting for this train that we must take, we have an idea who we will meet, where we're going or what experiences are ahead- we don't know all of the necessary or unnecessary stops in between here or there. So we blindly hop on board this long train and as we make our way through dozens or perhaps hundreds of train cars we witness festive parties that we thoroughly enjoy, we are seated at beautiful dinner tables with loved ones, we feel safe and secure in those settings. It's exciting, we can't wait to go in and visit the next car and the one after that and the one after that. We hurry ourselves along looking for a better time, more laughs, more of everything.

A short while later, we stumble into an empty, cold, dark car with just a splinter of light shining through cracks on the wall, we walk through other cars where people are suffering and some dying. We spend time in cars with angry, belligerent people who purposely hurt us. Realizing this pain, we anxiously make our way toward the conductor's car, hoping to get off this wild ride.

As we make that walk through more cars, we see the error of our ways in the faces of people we have hurt and we see our own reflection as we walk past those that have hurt us. We see the victories of ballgames and academic achievements and countless rejections that we interpreted as failure. We see the warmness of Christmas time with family and lots of gifts and we see the sadness of spending birthdays alone.

Fatigued and stressed out you finally approach the front car, you just want off the train at this point, you slide open the conductors door to find that no one is guiding the train, the spot is empty but the train is still moving. You see a sign: "Conductor on Duty: YOU". You suddenly realize that you have been guiding this train all along, carrying all of your past memories and baggage, living through old feelings and shame and unaware that you are really guiding your life by the choices you have made and by the intentions you set or lack thereof. You learn that this train ride isn't about the destination at all, it isn't about knowing where you're going or when it will stop, it's about the journey, the process of how you live during each moment. It's about how you live when times are high and cheer rings through your life, it's also about how you live through those darker moments when life feels dissolute and unrewarding.

The train ride is going to happen with or without your consent, you have a choice in how you live through it. Let tomorrow take care of itself, find splendor in the doing not the reward of the end result. These are precious days, precious breaths that signal our aliveness in the now. And I hope that is where you will always find your strut, purpose, power and position- right here, right here in the now, in the doing and the being. May God bless you and keep you.

END NOTES

Chapter 1- Where's My Stuff?

(The put downs)
Book Resource:
Chopra, Deepak, M.D, "Ageless Mind, Timeless Body", United States: Three
Rivers Press 1993

(I'm not sorry...for everything)
Internet Resource:
Karina Schumann and Michael Ross, "Why Women Apologize More Than
Men: Gender Differences in Thresholds for Perceiving Offensive Behavior",
Psychological Science Journal, November 10, 2010

Chapter 2- Resonate Reflection

(Strutting Stones)
Book Resource:
Hay, Louise, "You Can Heal Your Life", California: Hay House 1999,

Chapter 3- Preferential Pardon

(Forgive but keep it real)
Book Resource:
Schucman, Helen, "A Course in Miracles", New York, Viking: The Foundation of
Peace 1976

Chapter 4- Pacifying Poison People

(Why we stay)
Film Resource:
"Nights of Cabiria", 1957, Paramount Pictures

Chapter 5- Getting Unhazed

(beginning of chapter)
Internet Resource:
Herr, Norman, Ph.D, The Sourcebook for Teaching Science web site, "Television
& Health", undated statistics
http://www.csun.edu/science/health/docs/tv&health.html

Internet Resource:
William Adams, "Diane von Furstenberg on the Meaning of Luxury",
Time, June 17, 2010
http://www.time.com/time/arts/article/0,8599,1997006,00.html

(Draw your own conclusions)
Internet Resource:
Tony Dokoupil, "Is the Web Driving Us Mad?", Newsweek/The Daily Beast,
July 9, 2012
http://www.thedailybeast.com/newsweek/2012/07/08/is-the-internet-making-us-
crazy-what-the-new-research-says.html

(Draw your own conclusions)
Internet Protection Resource:
Leechblock
http://www.proginosko.com/leechblock.html

(What they won't tell you)
Internet Resource:
Christine Larorio, "Resources: Marketing to Kids", CBS News, February 11, 2009
http://www.cbsnews.com/2100-500823_162-2798401.html

(What they won't tell you)
Book Resource:
Tolle, Eckhart, A New Earth, United States: Penguin 2005

Chapter 6- Purposeful Living

(Shifting Gears)
Internet Resource:
Alexander Bird, "Thomas Kuhn", The Standard Encyclopedia of Philosophy,
August 13, 2004
http://plato.stanford.edu/entries/thomas-kuhn/

Chapter 7- Being Unreasonable and Unavailable

None

Chapter 8- Authority and Humility

(Noodle and Bone Crushing handshake)
Internet Resource:
"Gaddafi's Condoleezza Rice Photo Album Found At Tripoli Compound",
Huffington Post, August 25, 2011
http://www.huffingtonpost.com/2011/08/25/gaddafi-condoleezza-rice-album-
_n_936385.html

(Make Decisions Quickly)
Book Resource:
Hill, Napoleon, Think and Grow Rich, United States: The Random House
Publishing Group, Revised Edition 1960

(Say what you mean and mean what you say)
Internet Resource:
"Turning into Digital Goldfish", BBC News, February 22, 2002
http://news.bbc.co.uk/2/hi/1834682.stm

(Woman to woman)
Internet Resource:
Swami Sivananda, "Law of Retribution" The Divine Life Society, 2011
http://sivanandaonline.org/public_html/?cmd=displaysection&section_id=1160

(Woman to woman)
Magazine and Internet Resource:
Susan Adams, "Having a Woman Boss Doesn't Help Women Get Ahead", Forbes,
August 7, 2012
http://www.forbes.com/sites/susanadams/2012/08/07/having-a-woman-boss-
doesnt-help-women-get-ahead/

Chapter 9- Answering the 3 am Love Call

(Write new rules and exceed them)
Magazine/Internet Resource:
Don Yaeger, "The New 61", Success, June 2012
http://www.success.com/articles/1385-the-new-61

(Prayer and faith)
Television Resource:
Oprah Winfrey Interview, "The Next Chapter", June 10, 2012, OWN

Conclusion: Perfectly Positioned
Holy Bible- James 1:2-4 (New revised standard version)

RESOURCES

Dames Bond LLC

A professional networking organization that works to help women leverage the resources, connections, and marketing needed to thrive and prosper in business. Recognized by national magazines as one of the top ten career sites for women in business, DB is the first all-female professional organization purposefully designed to connect businesswomen with consumers and vice versa.

Dames Bond is an important step toward the collective power of positive social change for women. Women are strengthened by the dynamics of other women and desire an atmosphere where they can regularly connect with other women, on common ground. The greatest benefit comes from experiencing the support and sharing within a group.

There are three chapters and a nationwide business directory, for a chapter nearest you, check out their website.

Dames Bond, LLC
3500 N. High Street
Columbus, Ohio 43214
Phone: 614.209.3556
Website: www.damesbond.com
E-mail: info@damesbond.com

Landmark Education

An international training and development company that offers a variety of distinct programs that are built to empower individuals and assist them to move beyond personal limitations and existing views. Participants can choose among dozens of programs that cover many topics from personal growth to building better relationships and much more.

To learn more about the programs offered, visit the website.

Landmark Education
353 Sacramento Street Suite 200
San Francisco, CA 94111
Phone: 415.981.8850
Website: www.landmarkeducation.com

Margeau's "Free to Be" Project

Supports women and girls by building a strong sense of identity, resulting in a greater acceptance of oneself and a healthy and balanced approach to life. The project fosters authentic self-expression through creative activities and conversation. It nurtures relationships with other women and peers to promote positive self-esteem and counter feelings of self-doubt.

Margeau's "Free to Be" Project takes its name to honor 29-year old Margeau who died in 2011 after a long illness. The program founder says "Margeau was a remarkable woman who had a joyful spirit and saw the best in everyone, but struggled to see it in herself. Like many women Margeau suffered from feelings of inadequacy. Margeau's dream was to spare others from the demons she fought in her short life."

The project is dedicated to helping women and girls appreciate themselves and the gifts that they have to offer through raising awareness of various topics such as worth, value, inadequacy and more. Through an annual Day of Discovery, the program gives girls and women the tools needed to nurture their spiritual, physical and emotional needs

> Margeau's "Free to Be"
> Gail Stumphauzer, Director
> Northeast Ohio Area
> Phone: 440.561.2345
> Website: www.free2bproject.com
> Email: Gailstumphauzer@me.com

The Mustard Seed Foundation, Inc.

The Mustard Seed Foundation, Inc. (TMSF), is a nonprofit organization that offers transitional housing and supportive services to young women ages 13-21. TMSF accepts teen/young mothers who are in state or county custody or have been referred by other service agencies. It provides it's programs and services to all counties in Ohio.

The Mission of TMSF is to empower teens, youth and families to achieve their highest potential. Through education, prevention and advocacy TMSF works toward ultimately breaking the cycle of abuse and neglect and promoting family preservation.

The Vision of TMSF is to erase old thinking patterns and habitual cycles of generational poverty through supportive programs that teach parenting skills and building healthy, stable families. TMSF currently provides a variety of programs and services focused on four critical need areas:

- Residential
- Health/Wellness
- Outreach, Prevention & Awareness
- Positive Teen Development

TMSF was created by Shondale Atkinson, a product of Montgomery County Children Services who gave birth to her first daughter at the young age of 17. Due to lack of foster homes willing to house teen moms and their children, Shondale and her daughter were separated. It was because of this unfortunate situation that Shondale believes she was called to push TMSF into action. Her work has been cited in various newspapers, TV news stations, and she has been acknowledged as a community leader by some organizations. She is dedicated to TMSF's philosophy: "Faith to Grow a Brighter Tomorrow". For more information or to donate funds or volunteer, contact Shondale Atkinson.

The Mustard Seed Foundation, Inc.
Founder/Director of Operations
Shondale Atkinson
4880 Denlinger Rd.
Trotwood, Ohio 45426
Phone: 937.529.4010
Web site: www.themustardseedfoundationofdayton.org/home
E-Mail: info@themustardseedfoundationofdayton.org
        satkinson@themustardseedfoundationofdayton.org

National Council of Women's Organization

NCWO is a nonpartisan, nonprofit coalition of networks that address several needs and concerns of girls and women such as family and work, economic equity, education, corporate accountability, global progress for women's equality, and more. There are over 240 organizations representing more than 12 million women and NCWO is open to new members as well as support to help produce programs and other needs.

> NCWO
> 714 G Street SE, Suite 200
> Washington, DC 20003
> Phone: 202.293.4505
> Website: www.womensorganizations.org

SOAR

Provides innovative professional development programs for high-potential women (participants typically have 7-17 years of experience) who are prepared to advance within their organization or career. SOAR is rooted in a discussion-rich humanities-based curriculum with a strong mission to assist women in developing a unique style of leadership.

Its mission is to engage women in a journey of leadership self-discovery designed to help them identify their leadership strengths, challenges, and gaps and then create their own personal and professional leadership development plan. The SOAR program immerses members in a leadership curriculum rich in content and hands-on application that is designed to prepare them intellectually, psychologically, and skillfully for the tasks of leadership.

SOAR is expanding to other cities, check website for list of cities it currently serves.

> SOAR Headquarters
> 4344 Mt. Sterling Road
> Winchester, KY 40391
> Phone: 859.744.6521
> Website: www.seejanesoar.com

> For Greater Cleveland area SOAR interests:
> Roxanne Kaufman Elliott
> Phone: 440.653.9750
> Website: www.prolaureate-coaching.com/our-services
> E-mail: rkaufman@prolaureate.com

Transitional Housing INC.

Provide homeless women with a safe environment, programs and services to promote self-sufficiency and independence to end the cycle of homelessness. Programs include life management classes, workforce readiness services and family reunification programs. There is an 18 month period of follow up conducted once the client moves out of THI

Transitional Housing, Inc. (THI) was established in 1986 by three Catholic Sisters from the Congregation of St. Joseph. They founded THI in response to the serious shortage of safe, decent and affordable housing for low-income women living alone. They transformed a former motel on Cleveland's (OHIO) near West Side into what is now a 61-unit facility offering single room occupancy housing to low income women who are homeless.

Women may remain in the housing program for 12 months and pay a minimum monthly rent in exchange for their commitment to follow program rules which involve satisfactory completion of mandatory classes. The ten remaining rooms are permanent supportive housing units for women with chronic disabilities, who can stay with THI indefinitely.

THI was the first program of its kind in Ohio and one of the first transitional housing programs in the country. THI continues to be leading the charge as it recently has become certified as a Housing First program. Since its inception, THI has helped over 2,000 women break the cycle of homelessness and gain independence

> Transitional Housing INC.
> Sherri Brandon, Executive Director
> 1545 West 25th Street
> Cleveland, OH 44113-3158
> Phone: 216.781.2250
> Website: www.transitionalhousinginc.org
> Email: sbrandon@transitionalhousinginc.org

Toastmasters International

Toastmasters International is a nonprofit educational organization that operates clubs worldwide with the purpose of helping members achieve strong communication, public speaking and leadership skills.

There are over 280,000 members worldwide and participants can attend one of the 13,500 clubs in 116 countries that make up our global network of meeting locations. A Toastmasters meeting is a learn-by-doing workshop in which participants hone their speaking and leadership skills in a no-pressure atmosphere. There is no instructor in a Toastmasters meeting. Instead, members evaluate one another's presentations. This feedback process is a key part of the program's success. Meeting participants also give impromptu talks on assigned topics, conduct meetings and develop skills related to timekeeping, grammar and parliamentary procedure.

Guest are welcomed and membership fees are quoted at $36 every six months.

> Toastmasters International
> P.O. Box 9052
> Missing Viejo, CA 92690-9052
> Phone: 949.858.8255
> Web site: http://www.toastmasters.org

Author Note: (If in Cleveland, Ohio area, club # 351 is just one of the great clubs in the city and is conveniently located in downtown Cleveland.)

Women Donors Network

A national organization of proactive women that work together through collaboration and innovation for social change. As a network of progressive philanthropy, WDN is dedicated to enriching the lives of disadvantaged individuals and communities through programs and opportunities.

WDN leverages more than $150 million a year toward solutions that address the root causes of injustice and inequality. As a network of donors and donor activists, it offers opportunities to network with, learn from, and inspire one another.

> Women Donors Network
> 565 Commercial Street, Suite 300
> San Francisco, CA 94111
> Phone: 415.814.1333
> Website: www.womendonors.org
> E-mail: info@womendonors.org

Women in Business Networking

An organization for women in business that provides forums for
building relationships so women will achieve career and personal success
through education, resources and recognition. WiBN's circle of influence and
frequent programs have reached more than 1,500 women living and working
in the Greater Dayton, Ohio, region. Women from all walks of life participate
in WiBN: leaders and employees of corporate, nonprofit and community
organizations; entrepreneurs and small-business owners; and women in
career transition. Founded in 2008, WiBN currently offers several programs:

- Weekly e-newsletter, Monday Morning Moments

- Weekly club of Toastmasters International, Downtown Morning
  Toasters

- Monthly Lunch N Learn with a featured speaker

- Monthly "Hot Topic" Koffee Talk with a facilitator

- Monthly roundtables for small-business owners, Entrepreneur Groups;

- Master Mind Group with accountability partners

- Bimonthly social event, AfterGlow, at a local venue

- Quarterly Leadership Series workshop, Winstitute;

- Annual 25 Women to Watch recognition program

- Annual, daylong professional development conference…and more!

> President and Founder, Jeanne Porter
> Women in Business Networking
> 3072 Southdale Dr. #2
> Kettering, OH. 45409
> Phone: 937-470-4398
> Website: www.womeninbusinessnetworking.com
> E-mail: jporter@womeninbusinessnetworking.com

Women's Learning Partnership

An international nongovernmental organization that works to assist
women and girls through training curriculum and programs on leadership
and empowerment, organizational capacity building, human right, and

culture of peace. WLP promotes a model of participatory leadership that values the skills and contributions of every individual and emphasizes the important of collective action for gender equality and social justice

WLP also advocates and networks its efforts to ensure that the voices of women from the Global South, particularly Muslim-majority societies, are heard.

Women's Learning Partnership
4343 Montgomery Avenue, Suite 201
Bethesda, MD 20814
Phone: 301.654.2774
Website: www.learningpartnership.org
E-mail: wlp@learningpartnership.org

Raquel Eatmon

Author, Speaker, Journalist

P.O. Box 22153
Beachwood, OH 44122
www.RaquelEatmon.com

The work of Raquel Eatmon contributes to a stronger, kinder, gentler, more influential humanity with the intention of supporting others in living stronger lives--which can transform and heal our world. Raquel's approach to share her work through workshops, retreats, seminars, conferences, television, DVD's, and Internet are handled through our office. We organize requests that are in alignment with Raquel's methodology and principles.

www.RaquelEatmon.com
Raquel's official website

Connect:
Twitter: @RaquelEatmon
FaceBook: Raquel Eatmon (or) Woman of Power
LinkedIn: Raquel Eatmon

  Linked in

Made in the USA
Charleston, SC
20 February 2013